Mountain Bike Adventures in the

FOUR CORNERS REGION

Michael McCoy

The Mountaineers • Seattle

"Done with indoor complaints, libraries, querulous criticisms,
Strong and content I travel the open road."
——Walt Whitman, *Song of the Open Road*

The Mountaineers: Organized 1906 "... to explore, study, preserve, and enjoy the natural beauty of the outdoors."

Published by The Mountaineers
306 Second Avenue West, Seattle, Washington 98119

Published simultaneously in Canada by Douglas & McIntyre, Ltd., 1615 Venables Street, Vancouver, B.C. V5L 2H1

Manufactured in the United States of America

Edited by Miriam Bulmer
Maps by Carla Majernik
Cover photograph: The Colorado River from a four-wheel-drive road near Moab
All other photographs by Mike McCoy
Cover design by Betty Watson
Book layout by Bridget Culligan
Frontispiece: Riders take a break atop Gemini Bridge

Library of Congress Cataloging-in-Publication Data

McCoy, Michael, 1951–
    Mountain bike adventures in the Four Corners Region / Michael McCoy.
        p.   cm.
    Includes bibliographical references and index.
    ISBN 0-89886-251-5
    1. All terrain cycling--Four Corners Region--Guide-books.   2. Four Corners Region--Description and travel--Guide-books.
    I. Mountaineers (Society)   II. Title.
    GV1045.5.F68M37   1990
    746.6--dc20   90-40743
                                                                                          CIP

TABLE OF CONTENTS

Preface   9
Introduction   11

1. Arizona

Superstition and Mazatzal Mountains

   1. Tortilla Flat Out   32
   2. Pig City Loop   35
   3. Cottonwood Trailhead/Desert View   37

Payson

   4. The High Chaparral   39
   5. Cypress Thicket Loop   41
   6. Ride of the Purple Sage   43

Mogollon Rim

   7. Milk Ranch Point   47
   8. Coconino Roller Coaster   49
   9. Oak Hill Loop   50

Sedona–Jerome

  10. Red Rock Ramble   54
  11. Damfino Up from Down   56
  12. Mingus Mountain   58

Flagstaff–Grand Canyon

  13. Mount Elden Lookout Loop   61
  14. Cape Solitude Getaway   64

Other Rides in Arizona

2. Colorado

Grand Junction

  15. Bedrock Bash   71
  16. Lands End Loop   73

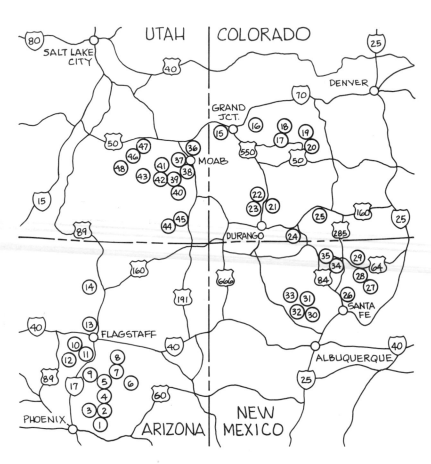

MAP SYMBOLS

——— PAVED ROAD	⬡ LOOKOUT
— — — GRAVEL ROAD	⅄ CAMPGROUND
········ TRAIL	◆ POINT OF INTEREST
— — — STATE LINE	) (MOUNTAIN PASS
—·—·— PARK BOUNDARY	■ RANCH OR CABIN
～···～·· RIVER/STREAM	⌶ FOREST SERVICE STATION
○ TOWN	※ MOUNTAIN OR KNOB

⬡ INTERSTATE	
⬚ U.S. ROAD	
○ STATE ROAD	
▭ FOREST SERVICE OR PARK ROAD	
★ START POINT	
➜ DIRECTION OF RIDE	

Crested Butte

17. Oh-Be-Joyful   76
18. Colorado Gothic   78
19. Teocalli Ridge Run   81
20. Cement Creek   84

Durango–Purgatory

21. Lime Creek Cliffhanger   85
22. Graysill Ghostbuster   87
23. Hermosa Creek Trail   91

Pagosa Springs–South Fork

24. Willow Draw Loop   95
25. High Lonesome Loop   97

Other Rides in Colorado

3. New Mexico

Santa Fe

26. Santa Fe Down   107

Taos

27. Macstas Ridge Climb   112
28. Rio Chiquito Bandito   114
29. Red River Valley   117

Jemez Mountains

30. Cochiti Splash   119
31. Bandelier Tough   122
32. Cerro Pelado Hill Climb   124
33. San Antonio Stroll   127

Brazos and Tusas Mountains

34. Spring Creek Cruise   129
35. Hopewell Ridge Loop   132

Other Rides in New Mexico

4. Utah

Moab

36. Willow Flats   140
37. Gemini Bridges   142
38. Hurrah Pass   144

Canyon Country

39.	Colorado River Overlook	148
40.	Anasazi Wonderland	151
41.	Panorama Point	154
42.	Lands End: The Sequel	157
43.	Dance with the Dirty Devil	158

Bluff–Mexican Hat

44.	Valley of the Gods Loop	163
45.	Comb Ridge Loop	165

Reef Country

46.	Little Wild Horse Whirl	170
47.	Temple Mountain Loop	173
48.	Cathedral Valley Loop	176

Other Rides in Utah

Appendices

A.	Recommended Reading	184
B.	Additional Map and Information Sources	187
C.	Mail-order Equipment	188

Index

PREFACE

In the early 1980s mountain biking was a young sport, pursued by a handful of pioneers on bikes primitive by today's standards. As we enter the 1990s, this undeniably American activity has gone mainstream and is among this country's most popular outdoor activities. Of the approximately 10 million bicycles sold in the United States last year, no fewer than 50 percent were of the fat-tire variety.

This guide is devoted to this new strain of fanatic fun addict. Thanks for letting me to tell you where to go.

Acknowledgments

Exceptionally helpful and/or encouraging when I was doing research for this guide were Donald Van Dariel, Dennis Roy, and Rodney Byers of the Tonto National Forest; Wilson Hunter, Jr., acting superintendent of Canyon de Chelly National Monument; acting superintendent John Reed and chief of interpretation John C. O'Brien, of Grand Canyon National Park; Arden Anderson of the Bureau of Land Management's Gunnison resource area office; Bob Lillie of the San Juan National Forest; Jimmy D. Taylor, superintendent of Colorado National Monument; Robert C. Heyder, superintendent of Mesa Verde National Park and Hovenweep National Monument; Brian Lloyd, Hal Knox, and Gene Tatum, of the BLM's Albuquerque district office; Janet Kurman, formerly of the Santa Fe National Forest; Edward J. Greene, supervisory park ranger at Bandelier National Monument; Russell W. Von Koch of the BLM's Moab district office; Larry Theivagt of the Fishlake National Forest; Karen Whitney and Phil Dendel, of Glen Canyon National Recreation Area; Paul Cowan, park ranger at Arches National Park; Martin C. Ott, superintendent of Capitol Reef National Park; and David K. Morris, acting superintendent of Canyonlands and Arches national parks and Natural Bridges National Monument.

Many others—both federal and state employees and private citizens—nominated routes for inclusion. Unfortunately, those rides fell beyond either the book's geographical scope or allotted research time, and will have to await inspection until volume 2 is in the works.

Thanks go to my longtime friend, Ramsey Bentley, and my always-been brother, Roger McCoy, who joined me, either collectively or individually, on several of the rides in Arizona, Colorado, and Utah. Willing and intrepid compadres, they would quietly roll with the flow when I'd blurt out something like, "Oh, by the way, tomorrow we have to drive 250 miles (half of it on gravel, most likely) to catch one more ride 40 miles south of Dumbsquat" (and they thought they were on vacation).

Finally, extra-special thanks to my wife, Nancy, to whom this book is dedicated. The only reason she didn't cover every inch of ground featured in the guide is because some of the research had to take place during the school year, when she's committed to the confines of her classroom. The rides she wasn't physically able to join me on, she accompanied in spirit.

INTRODUCTION

The Four Corners Region

The Four Corners Region is fast becoming mountain biking's mecca—a place to which a pilgrimage must be made at least once. Some of the rides here are the finest in the country, perhaps in the world. There are ample logging roads, jeep paths, and single-track trails—enough to keep even the most prolific route-finders occupied for years. This guide features 48 of the Four Corners Region's scores of top-notch rides.

A guidebook writer should use superlatives sparingly, or risk weakening their impact. But following this rule of thumb is tough when writing about the Four Corners Region. Trying to describe its glorious and unlikely landscape forces the "incredibles" and "spectaculars" to float from the pen like the bubbles on the surface of a slickrock waterhole.

In the geography of contrast surrounding the point shared by Arizona, Colorado, New Mexico, and Utah, you can begin driving in a lizard-filled, sun-baked June desert and an hour later stand atop a 10-foot snowbank while viewing vegetation similar to that found in the Arctic. The array of landforms and life zones staggers the senses and boggles the imagination.

The Four Corners Region cannot be simply defined; no government survey party has delineated its borders. To an extent, you must draw the boundaries as you see fit, for the area is partly a state of mind. Like the most equitable of map makers, you could elect to measure the region by the mile, so that the four sister states each contribute an identical acreage. You might choose to consider it in geologic terms, as do those who claim the Four Corners Region is that area encompassing the Colorado Plateau, a 150,000-square-mile uplifted tableland of wildly eroded sediments. Or you might side with those who define the region archaeologically—as containing this style of pottery and that type of cliff dwelling.

To me, the Four Corners Region is a blend of landscape, history, prehistory, geology, and proximity to the point shared by the four states. For this guide, the boundaries were drawn so that rides for all seasons could be included, and in as broad a selection of settings as possible. The result is a modest sampling of what's out there, a teaser. For each ride featured, two dozen more await discovery. Let this book be your key to unlocking additional mountain-biking secrets in the region. Pedal on the steep trails of southwest Colorado and on the finger-like mesas of northwest New Mexico; ride in southeast Utah's celebrated slickrock country and in the Sonoran Desert of Arizona. Follow the logging roads and old mining paths. Pedal fast sometimes and breathe hard, but stop occasionally to smell the desert and to hear the breeze whispering through the high-country spruce. Lie on a sandstone slab and take in the intense, hot sunshine. Walk through (only if permitted!) an ancient cliff dwelling and imagine living there. In this way you'll discover what the Four Corners Region means to you.

You'll better appreciate your mountain-bike travels here by reading some of the books listed in Appendix A. Learn about the geology and the Native Americans. Become familiar with the survival strategies of cacti and other desert flora, and of mountain wildflowers. Read of John Wesley Powell and his incredible travels down the Colorado River. Learn the meanings and pronunciations of Indian and Spanish place names: they're windows to the past, offering insights into the power of landscape and the depth of the early inhabitants' spirituality.

I strayed farther afield in the Grand Canyon State than in the others, for most of its northeast corner—nearly 20 percent of the state's acreage—is comprised of Navajo tribal lands. (The smaller Hopi Reservation is sandwiched inside the area, as well.) In this independent nation, larger than the state of West Virginia, travel off the main highways is discouraged. Technically, it is possible to obtain a backcountry permit for exploring tribal lands, but in the view of the *Diné* (the People), a family's traditional use of land will often supersede tribal ownership. Traveling down the wrong path—even one not fenced or posted—may be viewed as trespassing. For updated information, call Navajo Tribal Parks & Recreation in Window Rock, (602) 871-4941.

Mountain Biking: Where and Where Not to Go

Mountain bikes are not permitted on the trails in federal wilderness areas, with good reason. Bob Marshall, a pioneer of the American conservation movement, defined wilderness as "regions which contain no permanent inhabitants, possess no means of mechanical conveyance, and are sufficiently spacious for a person to spend at least a week of active travel in them without crossing his own tracks." If Marshall were alive today, he surely would agree that, as a mechanical conveyance that covers ground quickly, the mountain bike has no place on the trails in our treasured wildest places.

Like motorized trail bikes, mountain bikes are vehicles, though not as noisy or as potentially destructive to the terrain. Even on many trails where mountain bikes are permitted by law—most nonwilderness U.S. Forest Service trails, for instance—they often are not an appropriate means of travel.

When I am on my fat-tire bike, rolling through woods or desert, my senses sharpen. I cherish the scent of juniper and the sight of the setting sun casting its slanted rays on a forest of saguaro cacti, their outstretched arms waving "good night." But I also enjoy zipping along, particularly on the downgrades. I'm enjoying and appreciating nature, but at a much faster clip than when hiking. To many hikers and equestrians, a bicycle—especially one moving at a high rate of speed—is a mechanical intrusion.

By cycling in the areas featured in this guide, you will not only help avoid user conflicts, but also be riding on byways used by far fewer people than are many of the hiking and horseback trails. The latter often prove too steep and/or rocky for enjoyable mountain biking, anyway. In fact, the majority of the premier rides in the Four Corners Region take place on jeep and logging roads. The only *trail* riding recommended in this guide is on trails open to off-road vehicles (ORVs) and on those specially recommended by land administrators for mountain biking. Typically, these trails see little use by other recreationists.

Less conflict, fewer folks sharing the routes, and world-class rides—not a bad situation for the mountain biker.

Finding Your Way

How to use this book. The text is divided into four chapters, each detailing rides in one of the Four Corners states. At the end of each chapter is a summary of other suggested rides in that state. Appendix A features additional reading recommendations, Appendix B details map and information sources, and Appendix C suppliers of mail-order equipment.

Each ride is depicted on an accompanying map; in some instances, more than one ride appears on a single map. It is possible to accomplish the rides using this guide alone, but also consider carrying the recommended supplemental map for each ride. This book will be of little use for exploring pathways not featured, or for finding the way should you unintentionally get off course.

For each ride, the following information is listed:

Riding surface
Elevation range
Distance (round trip)
Relative difficulty (easy, moderate, or hard)
Time to allow
Best time of year for ride
Recommended supplemental map

The difficulty ratings obviously are somewhat subjective, but they do provide good guidelines. They are based on how I felt after doing each ride, and how others with me reacted to it. (Did they say, "Let's do it again!" or did they sprawl comatose for three hours on the desert floor?)

The ratings take into consideration both physical and technical challenges. A physically hard ride might be technically easy, or vice versa. For instance, a *downhill* stretch of loose sand can be technically tougher to negotiate than some of the steepest solid-surfaced uphills. And a physically hard ride might take place entirely on smooth dirt roads, dishing up no real technical challenges (other than that of avoiding a backwards somersault).

In some cases I have made suggestions on the best time of week to go. However, it's always best to check with the appropriate land administrators, for conditions may have changed since this book was researched. For example, on lands within the jurisdiction of the U.S. Forest Service and the Bureau of Land Management, resource-extraction operations can pick up or shut down at the drop of a hard hat.

Some commonly used abbreviations include: USFS (U.S. Forest Service), BLM (Bureau of Land Management), ORV (off-road vehicle), NRA (National Recreation Area), and WSA (wilderness study area).

Maps. A recommended supplemental map is listed in the information block preceding each ride description. The map—usually a USFS or BLM "visitors map"—typically contains a key indicating which U.S. Geological Survey topographic quadrangle maps cover the area. While these "topo" maps provide a wealth of detail about the terrain, you probably won't need one. The most recent edition might be 10 or 20 years old and thus not indicate all current roads and four-wheel-drive tracks, the very features most important to mountain bikers.

However, all riders should be experienced in using a topo map and compass, and you *should* utilize them when riding into areas not covered in this guide, where serious route finding may be required. Some of the books listed in Appendix A are good resources for learning the basics.

Road and trail signs. The signing of roads tends to be inconsistent at best and nonexistent at worst. Primitive roads on NPS lands typically are better signed—because visitors and their well-being are a top priority—than roads and trails on USFS and BLM lands.

Even when land managers do their best, efforts often are thwarted. Signs are defaced, stolen, and devoured by porcupines. A sign that was brand-spanking new and looked like a permanent fixture when a particular ride was researched may now be unreadable or adorning someone's bedroom wall. Always bear this in mind, and if your odometer and/or map and/or common sense indicate that you're at a certain point, but the sign mentioned in the narrative can't be located, believe the first three and give up the sign as gone.

Gearing Up

Your bike. If you are not already the proud owner of a mountain bike, there are several books that cover the basics: how to choose a bike, how to maintain it, what to look for when buying racks and packs, and so on. You'll learn a lot by perusing one or two of these books, regardless of your experience level. See Appendix A for suggestions.

Mountain cycling is more demanding than the paved-road variety, on both the body and the bicycle. Although fat-tire bikes are tougher than their skinny-tire counterparts, they require more maintenance. They tend to get dirtier, and nuts and bolts shake loose more often.

Wash your bike after a muddy or sandy ride and tighten any nut or bolt that looks like it's even *thinking* of coming loose. Keep the drivetrain—the chain, freewheel, chainwheels, and rear derailleur pulleys—clean and lubricated. Also, keep a light layer of grease on the inserted parts of the seatpost and the handlebar stem, to keep them from freezing to the frame. And regularly check the bottom bracket and headset: these are notorious for rattling loose on mountain bikes and could leave you literally up the creek in the outback if you are without the tools to re-tighten them.

Flat tires are the most common equipment failure experienced when mountain biking. Equipping your bike with high-quality, *fat* (between 1.9 inches and 2.125 inches) tires is the most effective way to limit the chance of flats, rim dents, sore neck muscles, and a host of other woes. To reduce import duties and provide prospective customers with a nimble test ride, mountain-bike manufacturers often slap 1.5-inch tires on their models. These are terrific for zipping around town or touring on pavement, but they're *too narrow* for all but the smoothest and driest conditions off pavement. In addition to flatting more often, narrow tires knife into soft surfaces, creating surface damage and difficult handling, and they dish out a much rougher ride.

Before each outing, inspect your tires, checking for cuts and abrasions and for foreign objects, such as cactus thorns, that have attached themselves to the sidewalls. If you plan to spend lots of time at the lower, desert elevations, consider using one of the widely available tire liners or liquid sealants to help reduce the chances of flats. Squeeze tires to see that they are adequately inflated. If they are not, down the road the tube may pinch between rim and rock, resulting in a flat tire and/or a dented rim.

Before heading out, you should also check to see if the brakes need adjusting: spin each wheel to see that it's clearing the brake pads, and make certain the pads are contacting the rim rather than the tire's sidewall.

At least once a year, advisably after the wet spring season, perform a complete overhaul or have your favorite shop do it. Repack all bearings in fresh grease, replace frayed cables, lubricate cable housings, and replace the chain and freewheel, if necessary. For performing a do-it-yourself overhaul, one of several books listed in Appendix A can lead you through step by step.

Most quality mountain bikes include bosses brazed onto the frame to accommodate two water-bottle cages. When buying a bike, ask the dealer to throw in a couple of cages and water bottles; many shops have bottles emblazoned with their logo, so you'll be advertising for them. If you already own a bike, be sure to add cages and bottles. Fill both bottles before heading out on even the shortest rides; for longer rides in hot weather pack along extra (full) water containers.

Toe clips, though not a necessity, do make pedaling more efficient: by "ankling" you'll gain power on the up stroke as well as the down stroke. They also hold feet in place on the rough stuff, resulting in fewer skinned shins. Strapless mini-clips are especially user-friendly, as they are easier to get out of in bail-out situations than clips with straps.

Many excellent packs and racks are made specifically for mountain bikes (see Appendix C for a list of equipment suppliers). A rear rack alone will do for day outings. However, the heavier loads necessary for an extended trip require both rear and front racks. Stowing gear into medium-capacity packs mounted fore and aft is preferable to cramming everything into large rear packs: the arrangement makes for easier packing and a better-balanced ride. For the front rack, stay away from "low riders." These are terrific for road touring but offer insufficient ground clearance for riding on uneven surfaces.

Odometers. Consider rigging an odometer a necessity. Several cyclocomputers available today are easy to hook up; they range in price from reasonable to rather expensive, depending on the options chosen. (Some of the newer models even incorporate elevation-measuring altimeters.) The essential features measure distance covered and elapsed time.

Mileages in the written narratives were measured to the nearest tenth of a mile. Because variations in size and pressure of tires and in individual odometers can produce different measurements over identical ground, your mileage readings may not always agree with those in this guide. But they should be close.

Bear in mind that the exact mileage on a mountain-biking route is often not as relevant as the amount of up-and-down or technical travel encountered. The combination of elevation changes and the wide spectrum of riding surfaces found makes it difficult to estimate the distance ridden. For example, after riding the Slickrock Trail near Moab, Utah, a mere 10.2 miles in length, first-timers may feel as though they have just finished a 100-mile ride... with a game of rugby thrown in for good measure.

Tools. The first axiom of mountain biking states that, sooner or later, you'll need to fix a flat. Practice the procedure at home under controlled conditions so that you aren't forced to learn it in the woods, in a rain- or snowstorm. Always carry along these tools:

* Frame-mounted pump
* Six-inch adjustable wrench
* Three tire irons
* Patch kit
* Spare tube

For repairs less likely, but well within the realm of fat-tire possibilities, add the following to your tool kit:

* Slot- and Phillips-head screwdrivers
* Allen keys
* Spoke wrench

* Four or five extra spokes
* Brake wrenches
* Chain lubricant
* One brake cable and one derailleur cable
* Chain-rivet remover
* Freewheel remover and pocket vise
* Small roll of electrician's tape
* Needle-nose pliers with cable cutter
* Assortment of nuts, bolts, and washers
* Assortment of hose clamps (the miracle fix-all)
* Adjustable pliers
* 6-inch locking-grip pliers
* Several bearings packed in grease in a film canister

The chances of needing most of these items are quite slim, especially if you've determined before heading out that everything is tight, full of air, or otherwise in good condition. But each can solve potentially big-time problems, so decide for yourself. The tools won't be of much use unless you know how to use them. While it's not in the scope of this book to detail mechanical matters, these tools and their uses are well described in several books listed in Appendix A.

Rooftop carriers. Deciding on which car-mounted carrying rack to buy can be nearly as tough as shopping for a bike. There are rooftop carriers, bumper "hanger" racks, trunk-mounted racks, and pickup-bed carriers. Some racks hold only two bikes, others as many as seven. In rooftop carriers alone, the options include carrying the bikes inverted, upright, and fork-mounted. (The last is the most stable, but requires removal of the front wheel.)

The roof is the least obtrusive and safest place to carry bikes, as long as the driver remembers not to pass under low-clearance overheads. Depending on the heights of the car and the cyclist, mounting the bikes on top can be a simple matter or it can require a stepladder. A rooftop carrier is the best choice for the multisport enthusiast, for many also accept adapters for hauling other toys, such as skis, canoes, and sailboards.

Shop around. The price range is wide (approximately $40 to $300), and the range of complexities great. For assembling some of the techiest of the high-tech racks, an advanced degree in mechanical engineering would be useful. The bumper- and trunk-mounted racks, historically cheap and unstable, have been improved dramatically in recent years. Still inexpensive, they make mounting and removing the bikes a relatively simple job, especially for the short of stature.

Your body. The *best* way to condition yourself for mountain biking is to ride daily in varying terrain. However, most folks can't ride every day, nor should they try. There's no better way to tire of something enjoyable than to feel obligated do it every day.

Instead, try to get in two or three rides a week for the several weeks leading up to your most active cycling season. The rides can be as long as desired and can take place on- or off-pavement, or even off-ground, on a wind trainer or stationary bicycle. At least at the beginning of the season, spread out your riding days as far from one another as convenient, so that your muscles can rebuild after unaccustomed demands.

Try to exercise at least five days a week, doing another form of workout you enjoy on the off-bike days. Anything—from soccer to skiing, walking to weight-lifting—will help prevent the muscle imbalances that can surface if cycling is your only exercise. You'll find that mountain biking begs for more upper-body strength than road cycling does, so exercise the upper as well as lower body.

You are your bicycle's motor. For optimum health and performance, add high-octane fuels to your body. Go easy on the fats and eat plenty of complex carbohydrates. When out for a day ride, bring carbos and fluids, and lots of them: fruit, gorp, leftover pizza, water, energy drinks, and so on. (Appendix A lists several books that will help you plan a nutritious and delicious diet.)

Clothing. The most comfortable and practical mountain-biking clothing is that designed for the sport. With the dazzling colors and designs available today, part of the sport's appeal is that it's possible to dress functionally like a wildman or -woman, yet retain a degree of social respectability.

If you plan to ride in clothes not specifically designed for cycling, avoid shorts and underwear with thick seams through the crotch, or you'll experience painful chafing on long and/or rough rides. One good combination is running shorts (preferably with a polypropylene liner) and a cotton T-shirt, but only for warm and dry weather; when it is cold and wet, wear wool or polypropylene.

As with specialized clothing, mountain-biking shoes are great, but lightweight, low-cut hiking boots serve just as well. Whatever footwear you choose, be sure that it's as appropriate for walking as it is for riding (leave the road-riding cleats at home).

To top off your outfit, don't leave home without an ANSI (American National Standards Institute) or Snell Foundation-approved hardshell helmet, eye protection, and leather cycling gloves.

Weather conditions may require extra clothing for even the shortest of rides. Some recommended foul-weather gear is listed in the Extended Overnight section.

Other essentials. A mountain bike will sweep you much farther away from civilization in a given period of time than foot travel will. And if, because of breakdown or accident, you're unable to pedal out the 20 miles you just rode in, you could be stuck in the backcountry with a heap of trouble on hand. Twenty miles is a long walk, especially when you are pushing a bicycle and the temperature is pushing a hundred.

Knowing where the potential for trouble lies will help keep you out of it. Stick the mountain biker's "10 Essentials" in your pannier or fanny pack, and be a well-prepared backcountry cyclist:

* Waterproof matches or butane lighter
* Compass and map of the area
* Pocket knife
* Extra water
* Extra food
* Raingear and warm clothing
* Flashlight or headlamp
* Plastic whistle
* Sunglasses
* Space blanket for body-heat retention

And *always* pack along a first-aid kit. Include:

* Two triangular bandages or large bandannas
* Assortment of gauze patches and adhesive strips (include butterfly closures, effective as temporary stitches)
* Moleskin for blisters
* Collapsible mini-scissors
* Spenco 2nd Skin (for burns, blisters, road rash)
* Adhesive tape
* Sunscreen (at least 15 SPF)
* Aspirin
* Three-inch elastic bandage
* Tweezers
* Baking soda for insect bites
* Insect repellent
* Antihistamine tablets (for allergic reactions)
* Two-inch gauze roll
* Antiseptic soap or small container of hydrogen peroxide

* Needles and thread
* Single-edge razor blade
* Antibacterial ointment
* Snake-bite kit
* Wire splint made from quarter-inch hardware cloth
* Instant cold-pack for sprains, strains, and broken bones

Stash the materials in a small, waterproof nylon tote or zip-seal freezer bag. Remember that, like tools, many of the items won't be of benefit if you don't know what they're for and how to use them. Become familiar with first-aid procedures by reading one of the books listed in the first-aid section of Appendix A or by signing up for a training course through your local Red Cross chapter.

Heading Out

Manners, manners. Bikecentennial, North America's largest recreational cycling organization, has generated a set of 10 rules known as the "Fat-Tire Commandments." The rules should be followed by all mountain-bike riders.

1. Stay on the designated travel corridor, and off the vegetation.
2. Yield right-of-way to slower and less-mechanized users.
3. Don't cut ruts: keep off muddy roads and trails.
4. Police your speed and ride in control.
5. Carry the 10 Essentials.
6. Tell a friend where you're going and when you'll return.
7. Respect trail closures and no-trespassing signs.
8. Leave gates as you found them.
9. Practice minimum-impact travel and camping.
10. Help teach new riders the proper trail etiquette.

Remember, other mountain bikers will be judged by your actions.

Horse sense. A word on horses: the Four Corners Region is cowpoke country, and sooner or later you'll run across saddle or pack animals on the trail. Horses are skittish—some will spook and bolt merely at the snapping of a branch. When approaching stock, from either the front or rear, dismount and push your bicycle. If possible, pass on the lower side of the trail, because the horses will be easier to round up if they bolt uphill rather than downhill. Talk to the horse and rider so the horse knows you're human and not some alien, two-wheeled life form. Bear in mind that pack horses spook more easily than horses with riders. Don't let an encounter result in a runaway pack horse!

Go easy on the land. The desert may look harsh and tough, but it's sensitive to abuse. In some desert areas of the Four Corners Region, you'll find *cryptogamic* soil, a crusty conglomerate of lichens, algae, and mosses. Important to other plant species because it fixes nitrogen and holds water, seeds, and soil, cryptogam is fragile and slow to recover after being damaged.

Also sensitive are the high meadows and alpine tundra. No matter what the setting, if a feature you want to visit is not reachable by road or legal trail, stash your bike and hoof it. Fat tires will cut ruts in cryptogam and smash wildflowers and compact the oftentimes barely adequate topsoil found in the high country.

Riding technique. The best way to learn mountain bike handling is to ride in varying terrain. Keep the basics in mind, and your learning will be smoother.

Fit. If you already own a mountain bike, there's not much you can change here. But if you are new to the sport and shopping, or if you're thinking of trading up soon, consider this: in order to develop and enhance technique, a bike must fit properly. If you believe the mountain bike you're test riding fits perfectly because it feels just like a road bike, you're dead wrong. If it seems about three sizes too small—sort of like a kid's toy—you're getting warm.

When you straddle a mountain bike with your feet planted flat on the ground, there should be four to five inches of clearance between the top tube and your crotch. The long seat stem will provide the necessary leg extension, which should be a bit less than on a road bike—that is, you should have slightly more bend in your knees when pedaling, to aid with shock absorption.

Going up. Learn to use your bike's gears. To reduce knee wear, always spin the pedals *at least* 60 complete revolutions per minute (highly skilled riders find it most efficient to spin at a cadence of 80 to 110 RPM). Try sitting down; then try standing on the pedals, with weight either forward over the handlebars or backward over the seat, depending on the terrain. The subtle weight shifts necessary to adjust to changing terrain take practice to comprehend and accomplish effectively.

Going down. Learn to brake, lean into corners, and stay loose. Don't overuse the front brake, or you'll suddenly become an honorary member of the OTB (Over-the-Bars) Club. Regardless, you'll likely be initiated into this club sooner or later, and when you least expect it. Prepare by wearing a helmet on *every* outing. This will help see you through the induction ceremony in good order.

"Feather" the brakes on downhills, pumping them gently to control speed. If an all-out emergency stop is necessary, shift your weight back and apply the rear brake slightly more than the front (on the flats, apply both brakes equally). On extremely steep downhills stand slightly, move your weight back over the rear tire, and squeeze the seat between your thighs for stability. Practice braking and skidding the front and rear tires in controlled situations, and you'll develop the skill for braking under surprise conditions. (Do this on a dry gravel road, and never at the expense of a sensitive tread surface.)

Letting some air out of your tires for the rough, rocky downhills will soften the ride. Don't overdo it; you'll risk flat tires and dented rims if they get too mushy. For better shock absorption, keep relaxed in the upper body, with your elbows slightly bent, while maintaining a firm— but not tense—grip on the handlebars. And take advantage of your bike's quick-release adjuster for saddle height. Dropping the seat on long downhills enhances stability by lowering the center of gravity and also puts you in more immediate touch with the ground, should a dab of the foot be needed to maintain balance.

Cornering. Turn not by steering with the handlebars, but by leaning into the corner: you'll then automatically steer through it with weight properly distributed. Keep the inside pedal at the top of the revolution. Keeping the outside pedal down and weighted serves two purposes: the inside pedal won't catch on the ground and cause a wipe-out, and traction will be improved.

When approaching a sharp curve, first check your speed by sharply applying both brakes. Then, entering the turn, let up on the front brake and favor the rear one while accelerating through the corner.

Read the coming terrain. Get in the habit of looking 50 to 100 feet ahead so you're prepared to downshift, brake, or get up and out of the saddle at the appropriate time. This practice will help make your riding smooth and efficient. Look ahead at the line you want to take, for the bike naturally follows your line of sight. (Likewise, by looking where you *don't* want to go—such as over an adjacent cliff—you may end up going there.)

The Extended Overnight

What to bring. Aside from bicycle tools, packing for an extended mountain-bike outing is similar to preparing for a backpacking trip. The following list includes items needed for a multiday, high-elevation trip. Judge for yourself what to leave at home if, for example, you're going out only for an overnight and will not encounter high elevations and/or unpredictable weather. Add to and subtract from this list as your experience grows. (A packing tip: roll your clothes into tubes, place them in clear plastic bags, and pack them vertically in your packs so the ends are visible.)

* Rainsuit/windsuit
* Long wool pants for campwear
* Polypropylene/Lycra-blend tights
* Warm sweater or polyester fleece jacket
* Lightweight wool sweater or wool shirt
* Wool or polypropylene mittens or gloves
* Wool or polypropylene stocking cap
* Spare lightweight shirt and underwear
* Athletic shoes for campwear and stream crossings
* Waterproof shoe covers
* Bathing suit
* Down- or synthetic-filled sleeping bag
* Sleeping pad
* Lightweight tent
* Backpacking stove, cook set, and eating utensils
* More food than you'll need
* Toiletries: toothbrush, soap, and so on
* Three or four elastic bungee cords

Camping. When camping, always think *no trace*. Avoid camping on delicate alpine meadows and desert cryptogam. Choose instead sandy, pine-needle-strewn, or slickrock surfaces. If you set up a multiday camp in an area of vegetation, move your tent daily in order to avoid killing the flora lying under the tent floor.

Pack out what you pack in, and more. You'll rarely have trouble finding a little extra trash left behind by the less thoughtful.

A word on weather. Weather in the Four Corners Region is as varied as the topography. Extremes in temperature—at the top and the bottom of the thermometer, depending on season and locale—are common. Moreover, rapid *daily* change in the weather should be anticipated. It's possible to begin riding under cloudless skies in the morning, only to be drenched by rain or snow in the afternoon. Regard the equipment and tool lists seriously, and you'll be prepared for whatever the fickle weather gods deal out.

And use common sense. If you awaken at 7:00 A.M. under clear, Arizona-desert skies in June and it's already 75 degrees, don't head out on a 30-mile ride. It may be 115 degrees by the halfway point where, to make matters worse, you're sure to run out of water. Conversely, especially in spring and fall, check the weather forecast before departing on a long trip into the high country. If the weather is predicted to turn nasty, revise plans and stay low.

Because of the wide range of elevations and corresponding weather conditions in the Four Corners Region, the optimum riding months vary from route to route. Use this general chart only for a guideline; check with the local land administrators for current conditions.

Elevation	Optimum Riding Months
1,000–3,000 feet	October through April
3,000–5,000 feet	February through May; September through November
5,000–8,000 feet	April through November
8,000–12,000 feet	June through September

Conditions will vary from year to year and place to place. You might be able to ride in April at 9,000 feet near Flagstaff, but not until June at that elevation in parts of Utah or Colorado. At elevations of 11,000 to 12,000 feet in Colorado, routes may not be snowfree until well into July.

Of course, a ride at 2,000 feet in elevation can be done in July— even fairly comfortably—if it's not too long and is begun at first light of day. But you can't, no matter how ambitious you are, successfully complete in January a ride at 10,000 feet. An 8-foot snowpack just doesn't provide adequate traction.

Staying Healthy

Health problems in the desert or mountains often are a direct result of the weather and/or elevation, and an individual's lack of preparedness for them.

Hypothermia. Hypothermia, or exposure, is a lowering of the body's core temperature. It can lead to collapse and death and is, in fact, the leading killer of outdoor recreationists. To avoid hypothermia, stay warm and *dry.* Dress and undress in layers, striving to maintain a point of equilibrium where you're neither cold nor sweating profusely and thereby compounding the problem by dampening clothes and becoming overly dehydrated. Wear a light wicking (nonabsorbent) layer, such as polypropylene, directly against your skin, and drink plenty of fluids. Most hypothermia cases occur at between 30 and 50 degrees Fahrenheit, so it's a very real threat when cycling in the mountains, especially with the increased wind chill effected by riding at high speeds. Exhaustion adds to the problem, so get plenty of rest and don't go at it too hard.

Heat-related disorders. Succumbing to exposure while pedaling in the Sonoran Desert in July is unlikely. But the body's temperature-regulation system can run drastically afoul in hot weather also, resulting in hypothermia's hot-weather counterpart, hyperthermia. When your body accumulates more heat than it can dissipate, heat exhaustion and the more serious heat stroke can result. Heat cramps, less worrisome but still potentially immobilizing, can occur during bouts of heavy sweating.

If the day is going to be a hot one, start riding at first light, so that you're finished by midmorning. If you want a long ride, head to higher ground and save the low-country riding for a cooler season. If you do decide to forge ahead into dangerously hot conditions, carry a tarp and tent poles for makeshift shade. In the desert, natural shade can be as hard to locate as water.

At any elevation, when the sun is out, cover up with lightweight clothes and/or sunscreen, and drink water, then more water. In the extremely low relative humidities common in the region, you'll sweat more than at higher humidities but won't sense it—sweat quickly evaporates into the dry, thirsty air before it has a chance to dampen skin or clothing.

Remember: conserve sweat, not water. In moderately hot conditions drink from *four to six quarts* of water during a full day's outing to keep adequately hydrated. Drink before, during, and after exercise. And include a large proportion of carbohydrates in your diet: carbos stored in body cells retain water in much greater quantities than stored fats, which retain almost no water.

Altitude sickness. If you're not accustomed to them, elevations of 7,000 to 12,000 feet can cause symptoms such as loss of appetite, nausea, and headaches. If you're coming from the lowlands, at the least you'll experience shortness of breath and lack of energy. Acclimate gradually to the higher elevations by spending two or three days in the 5,000- to 6,000-foot range before heading to the really high country. To help limit the effects of high altitude, drink plenty of water, eat lots of energy-producing food, and don't push too hard at first.

Lightning. During summer, heat rising from the ground surface forces moisture high into the sky, where immense cumulus clouds build. The colder temperatures at these elevations, often in excess of 20,000 feet, cause condensation to occur. Then rain can take place, sometimes in the form of intense cloudbursts. These rains and accompanying violent thunderstorms are most common in July and August, in both the desert and the high mountains. Generally, it's a good idea to finish riding before 1 P.M. and return to car or camp before thunderheads have an opportunity to grow boomingly large.

If you find yourself along a ridgetop during a lightning storm, run, ride, or roll off it as quickly as possible. To get caught in one of these slam-bammers is to learn the true meaning of fear. In addition to ridgetops, avoid lone trees, open areas, shallow caves, and the bases and edges of cliffs. Safer locations include deep caves, heavily forested terrain, and beneath and between big rocks in boulder fields. In desert areas, don't seek out arroyos (dry washes) for sanctuary, as flash floods could race through in a solid wall of water. The torrents can occur even if it's not raining immediately where you're located.

Summer lightning storms often pass in less than an hour, so sit tight and enjoy the rest break. If you absolutely cannot claim safer ground, here's what the USFS recommends: sit on a small rock with insulating material, such as a foam pad or a pack, under you with only your buttocks and feet touching the rock, and your hands clasped around your knees. If you *are* struck, the lightning bolt might not pass through your heart, thanks to the insulation.

Other Safety Concerns

Creepy crawlies. The danger of being bitten or stung by snakes, spiders, and bugs is usually overstated. However, there are a few critters you should keep an eye out for while traveling in the Four Corners Region, especially at the lower, desert elevations. Rattlesnakes are the number-one concern. Here are four rules to help keep you bite-free:

1. Don't stick hands or feet into places you can't see, such as rock overhangs.
2. Use a flashlight when walking about at night.

3. Move slowly through undergrowth, giving any nearby snake the chance to skedaddle.

4. Don't handle a snake whether it's alive *or* dead. Reflex actions can cause it to strike even if the head is severed from the body.

Other poisonous animals residing in desert areas of the region include gila monsters, large, sluggish, and mostly nocturnal lizards found in the U.S. only in Arizona; scorpions, often located under rocks and among piles of debris; black-widow spiders; and centipedes. Another poisonous reptile, the coral snake, is found in the Sonoran Desert, but is subterranean and rarely seen. In general, the rules for avoiding rattlesnakes are adaptable to sidestepping confrontations with the other animals.

Wood ticks, potentially disease carrying, are found in parts of the region. When riding through grassy or brushy areas wear light-colored clothing so ticks can be spotted; tuck pant legs into socks and shirt into pants; inspect yourself and your companions' backsides often; wear repellents, especially around shoes, socks, and cuffs; and thoroughly inspect your head and body when returning from a ride. Ticks crawl around looking for choice diggings, and seldom attach themselves during the first few hours.

If you are bitten by a wood tick, remove it as soon as possible. The suggested procedure is to grab the tick with small tweezers as near to your skin as possible, and gently pull it out. Try not to crush it, as its juices may contaminate the wound. Save the tick in a jar in case health officials need it later for identification purposes. If, at any time during the next couple of weeks, you develop a rash or flu-like symptoms, consult a doctor at once.

Bad water. The days are gone when we could confidently stick a cup into a mountain stream for a nice, cold, *healthy* drink of water. The one-celled animal known as *Giardia lamblia* is present in many cold and apparently pristine surface waters. Deposited in or near streams via animal droppings and human waste, the waterborne cyst is ingested by drinking from the open water. After entering the body the cyst attaches itself to the intestine wall, where body heat activates it into its reproductive, or trophozoite, stage.

If you are susceptible to this bug, you'll get sick about two weeks later—long enough after drinking the tainted water that you may not think to blame the mountain stream for your ill health. The primary symptoms of giardiasis are severe diarrhea and nausea, which can last for months if not treated.

There are two effective and relatively simple ways to purify open water: heat it to boiling or filter it through an approved filtration device. Filtering is the more convenient method of purification and it won't affect the water's taste as boiling will.

(Lest we think it was created simply to give recreationists a pain in the gut, recent research indicates that *Giardia lamblia* has been around for no fewer than 3.5 billion years—long before there were any guts to inhabit. It may have been the earth's first organism with a nucleus, and an important step in the evolution from one-celled to more complex multicelled animals, such as ourselves.)

To avoid adding to the problem of polluted waters, adopt the "cat method" of human waste disposal. Always carry a digging tool, such as a long knife blade. Select a spot at least 150 feet from the nearest water, and in the timber or brush, if possible, avoiding damp and boggy areas. Dig a hole 6 to 8 inches square, and try to remove any existing sod in one piece. After use, burn the toilet paper (in the hole), fill the hole with loose soil, and tamp in the sod. Nature will see to the rest.

Hunting season. The big-game hunting season varies from state to state; throughout the autumn months folks will be shooting at animals in one or another of the Four Corners states. The woods and scrublands aren't as dangerous as some might imagine, but still it's a good idea to dress in bright colors—perhaps don a blaze-orange hunter's vest—and to make more noise than usual, in case a Nimrod is stalking around the next bend. Often more hunters are out during the first few days of the season than later on.

Solo travel. Riding alone can be an enlivening experience. You'll see, hear, and smell more acutely than when riding with others. But going solo means taking full responsibility for your actions and being doubly prepared for any emergency situation. Always tell a friend where you're headed and when you'll return. If a search party must be dispatched, the chances of finding you will be much greater if they know the general area you were riding in. Take the equipment lists seriously when riding alone, especially into more remote areas. Think ahead and imagine yourself in various situations, then prepare for them. Don't be caught asking, "Oh, great—what do I do now?"

Fatigue. As in skiing and other activities requiring good balance and sharp motor skills, mountain-biking accidents occur more frequently when the rider is worn out. To avoid extreme fatigue, eat plenty of food and drink lots of water throughout the day, and take frequent rest breaks. When approaching the end of a long day, avoid the temptation to ride fast over the sort of tricky sections you were able to negotiate earlier, when fresh. Fatigue breeds sloppiness, and when tired you're much more apt to catch a pedal on a rock or slide a tire on loose gravel than when fresh.

A word of warning. No doubt about it, mountain biking in the mountains and desert is a risk sport. In 1989 two mountain bikers died in the Moab area—one from a long fall and the other from exposure to the elements. Simply because a route is featured here doesn't mean that it's safe for all riders. The routes vary in difficulty and in the amount of training and equipment needed to enjoy them safely.

A route, or the status of its signing, may have changed since it was inspected. And conditions can change, even day to day, as a result of weather and other factors. A trip that is safe in good weather or for a well-equipped rider in top condition may be unsuitable in nasty weather or for someone not properly trained or equipped.

Don't let these warnings scare you off. Hundreds of folks enjoy safe cycling excursions throughout the Four Corners Region each year. However, they do accept this: an element of the beauty, freedom, and excitement of mountain bicycling is the presence of risks not encountered at home. Assume these risks and enhance your safety by being knowledgeable, prepared, and alert.

There's not space in this guide to describe everything one needs to know before traveling into remote areas, but a number of good books (see Appendix A: Recommended Reading) and public courses on the subjects are available. Take advantage of them to increase your knowledge.

Enough lecturing. Let's go have some Four Corners, fat-tire fun!

1
ARIZONA

Arizona's landscape, astonishing in its variety, ranges from the low-lying Sonoran Desert to the 12,000-foot San Francisco Peaks and to the state's nick-namesake, the Grand Canyon, among the most spectacular sights on earth. The following rides are centered around five locations: the Superstition and Mazatzal mountains, the town of Payson, the Mogollon Rim, the Sedona-Jerome area, and the Flagstaff-Grand Canyon vicinity. (Note: some of Arizona's featured areas are quite far from the point where the Four Corners states meet; see note concerning this in the Introduction.)

Superstition and Mazatzal Mountains

When first glancing at a map of this area that lies immediately east of the out-of-control sprawl of Phoenix, you might think the mountain-biking possibilities are endless. On closer inspection, however, you would note that much of the country is within the Superstition and Four Peaks wilderness areas and as such is off-limits to fat tires.

Even in nonwilderness areas, the majority of the old mining roads found in the ranges are prohibitively steep. Unlike the logging roads common in forested mountain ranges, with their constant 6- to 8-percent pitch (the grade a loaded logging truck can handle over distance), mining roads seem to have been designed with one goal in mind: to get from here to there the shortest way possible, come hell or high ridgetop.

These are desert mountains, best avoided in summer. Regardless of the season, carry plenty of drinking water when riding here. For base camps, several USFS campgrounds are located along the banks of the nearby reservoirs, such as Apache and Theodore Roosevelt lakes. But remember, the largest "tree" you're likely to find is a saguaro cactus (the bloom of which is Arizona's state flower), providing shade both skinny and scarce.

Tortilla Flat, Arizona, along the Apache Trail

For a lesson on the local ecology and an up-close, personal look at some prehistoric cliff dwellings, drop by Tonto National Monument, located roughly halfway between rides 1 and 2 on the Apache Trail. (A National Forest Scenic Byway, the Apache Trail itself makes a splendid mountain-bike route during low tourist counts.) Also, keep an eye out for the legendary Lost Dutchman gold mine: you may be getting warm!

The supplemental map, the Tonto National Forest visitors map, is available through the Forest Supervisor's Office, 2324 East McDowell Road, Phoenix, AZ 85010, (602) 225-5200, and at district offices in Carefree, Globe, Mesa, Payson, Young, and Roosevelt.

1. Tortilla Flat Out

Riding surface: Sandstone, smooth dirt, river cobbles
Elevation range: 2,882 to 3,190 feet
Distance: 6.3 miles
Relative difficulty: Easy
Time to allow: 1 to 2 hours
Best time of year: October through April
Supplemental map: Tonto National Forest visitors map

Study the visitors map, and note that this old jeep track, designated Forest Road 213, occupies a narrow finger of nonwilderness land jutting into the Superstition Wilderness. It makes for a short but fun

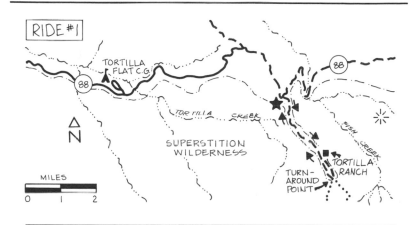

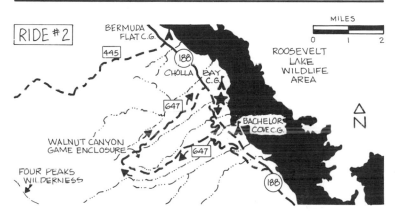

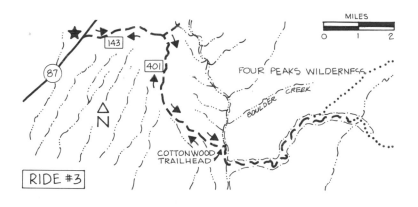

ride, good any day, and presents rewarding desert vistas. Do the ride early in the morning or at dusk, and watch the desert come alive with American cardinals, lizards, jackrabbits, mule deer. Listen for the haunting call of the mourning dove, the mocking of the raven, and the low, twittering monotone of the ubiquitous cactus wren.

From Apache Junction, at the eastern edge of Phoenix's urban spread, go northeast on State Highway 88/Apache Trail. Winding up, down, and around classic John Wayne, head-'em-off-at-the-pass canyons, roll through Tortilla Flat at 17.7 miles (there's nothin' flat about it!). There's a USFS campground here. At 23.2 miles the pavement ends; drive 1 mile beyond to the Tortilla Trailhead and park to the right.

Walk or ride steeply uphill on sandstone bedrock for about 200 yards. Don't let the intro to this route scare you off, as it does all but the most intrepid of motorists. It's the most difficult stretch on the entire outing. At 0.5 mile cross over a little saddle, and at 0.7 bear left; look

Superstition Mountains landscape

over your shoulder and mark this point in your mind, for it's a bit more confusing when coming from the other direction.

At a saddle at 1.6 miles, pass through a high gate in the fence and start down. At 2.4 pass through the old Tortilla Ranch site, replete with corrals, foundations, and windmill. Bear right at the Y; encounter some rough riding on river cobbles at 2.6. At 2.9 arrive at the Superstition Wilderness boundary and a spring site with a windmill. Curve left and circle around, reversing direction.

At 3.1, on the right, is a more prominent wilderness trailhead. At 3.7 you loop back to the ranch site; backtrack to the beginning point, regained at 6.3 miles.

2. Pig City Loop

Riding surface:	Smooth dirt with rocky stretches
Elevation range:	2,150 to 3,716 feet
Distance:	7.8 miles
Relative difficulty:	Hard
Time to allow:	2 to 3 hours
Best time of year:	October through April
Supplemental map:	Tonto National Forest visitors map

This ride encircles an expanse of chain-link fence, incongruously winding up and down a pair of otherwise pristine desert ridges. The fence marks the boundaries of the Walnut Canyon Game Enclosure. The mile-square, predator-free—from predators incapable of flight, at least—enclosure was established by the USFS and the Arizona Game and Fish Department for studying the habitat needs, population dynamics, and pathology of mule deer and javelina.

The unlikely looking and fast-moving javelina (the Spanish "j" is pronounced as an "h"), also known as the collared peccary, is North America's only native wild pig. You have a good chance of spotting some early in the morning or at dusk; you may detect their musky odor before seeing them.

From the Roosevelt Lake dam (built in the early 1930s and the tallest masonry dam in the world), at the junction of State Highway 88/Apache Trail and State Highway 188, go north on 188 for 5 miles and park at Cholla Bay Campground. (Note: Bermuda Flat Campground, 2 miles north of here, is a somewhat nicer campground than Cholla Bay. Three-Bar Road/Forest Road 445 shoots up into the hills opposite the campground, offering an intriguing "yo-yo" ride.)

Pedal uphill out of Cholla Bay Campground, circling under and

Theodore Roosevelt Lake, impounded by the world's tallest masonry dam

turning right (south) onto State Highway 188 at 0.1 mile. At 0.4 turn right toward Bachelor Cove Campground; head straight onto Forest Road 647 rather than left into the campground. At 0.8 pass through a deep cut and begin a gentle downgrade. At 1.4 turn right off the boulder-blockaded road onto a primitive path that soon presents some very steep, walking-advised (or necessary) upgrades.

At 2.2, passing a sign explaining the game enclosure, join the fence on its drastic ridge ascent. The chain link of the fence is echoed in an abundance of chainfruit cholla growing along the ridge. At 2.9 miles begin circling the head of the canyon; the namesake mountains of the Four Peaks Wilderness are laid out immediately in front. If it's spring, you'll enjoy the sweet scent of honey mesquite trees, as do the thousands of buzzing bees.

At 3.7 miles encounter a steep "walker" that persists for about 300 yards. Top out at 4.1 and switchback right as a more primitive trail forks left. Gaze down at Roosevelt Lake and at the fenceline you're still paralleling; spanning whatever it encounters, it looks like the Great Wall of Arizona.

At 4.7 miles bear left away from the fenceline, and at 4.9 continue on the same road as a more primitive path forks left into the adjacent arroyo. Keep crankin' on those brakes, and pass through a forest of saguaro giants in the 5.2-mile vicinity. At 7.0 miles turn right onto State Highway 188; at 7.6 turn right, returning to Cholla Bay Campground. At 7.8, back at the beginning point, jump into Roosevelt Lake and cool off. A hand massage might be in order as well, after trying to control your speed on the Pig City Loop descent.

3. Cottonwood Trailhead/Desert View

Riding surface:	Smooth gravel
Elevation range:	1,900 to 2,728 feet
Distance:	14 miles
Relative difficulty:	Easy
Time to allow:	2 to 3 hours
Best time of year:	October through April
Supplemental map:	Tonto National Forest visitors map

This straightforward little outing follows a baby-bottom-smooth road to the Cottonwood Trailhead entrance into the Four Peaks Wilderness Area. Accomplishable by folks of all skill levels, it presents terrific closeups of the desert and views of the Four Peaks. Because the road is so smooth and relatively close to the city, you might encounter substantial amounts of motorized traffic on weekends; weekdays are best.

On the visitors map note the nonwilderness, primitive-road corridor jutting eastward from the Cottonwood Trailhead into the Four Peaks Wilderness, looking much like the situation on ride 1. However, this jeep trail, nowhere near as tame as the road followed on the Tortilla Flat Out, climbs into the mountains at an impossible pitch.

From Mesa, go north/northeast on State Highway 87. After 30 miles, pass the turnoff to the Bush Highway/Forest Road 204, which heads south to Saguaro Lake. Continue straight on Highway 87 for 4 miles, and park at the right-hand turnoff to Forest Road 143.

Pedal eastward on Forest Road 143, the early stretches of which may be quite washboarded. At 0.8 mile cross a cattle guard; in a generally upward trend, the road dips and rises toward the mountains as it traverses the geographical feature known appropriately as "The Rolls." At 2.6 miles turn right onto Forest Road 401 toward the Cottonwood

Sonoran Desert view

Trailhead. (Note: a left turn leads to Lone Pine Saddle and eventually over the mountains and down to State Highway 88, at a point 6 miles north of the Pig City Loop. This would be a long and arduous ride; inquire at the Mesa Ranger Station before attempting it.)

Pass through a cow camp at 3.1 and continue over the rolling terrain. At 6.2 begin the steep descent into the trailhead area, reached at 7.0. The artifacts at this old cattle outpost include corrals, a bunkhouse, a cattle-loading chute, and a windmill and reservoir.

Heading up and out, retrace your tracks back to the beginning, while you look at the other side of everything you saw when riding in.

Payson

Payson, an idyllic little town, lies midway in elevation between the low desert and the 7,000-foot-high Mogollon Rim. Since 1970 the community has grown from 3,000 to 7,500 residents, as retirees discover that when it's hot in the Phoenix and Tucson areas—half of the year or more—temperatures are pleasant at Payson's 5,000-foot elevation. Likewise, when the Rim and towns such as Flagstaff to the north are buried in snow, Payson's occasional winter dustings typically melt by mid-afternoon.

As you huff and puff up the hills surrounding Payson, appreciate that you're inhaling some of the world's healthiest air. Payson's chamber of commerce brags that *Sunbelt Retirement* magazine named the Pine-Payson area as one of only three spots in the world with pure air ozone belts (whatever that means). A recreational paradise, Payson is gateway to the 250,000-acre Mazatzal Wilderness, to the wild and scenic Verde River, and to the expanses of the vast Mogollon Rim.

In addition to those featured below, many other good mountain-bike outings exist in the area. Poke around and you'll uncover some gems. The supplemental map needed for the Payson vicinity is the Tonto National Forest visitors map, available through the Forest Supervisor's Office, 2324 East McDowell Road, Phoenix, AZ 85010, (602)225-5200, and at district offices in Carefree, Globe, Mesa, Payson, Young, and Roosevelt.

4. The High Chaparral

Riding surface: Smooth gravel, embedded cobbles
Elevation range: 3,032 to 4,200 feet
Distance: 10.6 miles
Relative difficulty: Easy
Time to allow: 2 to 3 hours
Best time of year: February through May, September through
                    November
Supplemental map: Tonto National Forest visitors map

This route climbs a ridge rising toward the Mazatzal Mountains, and passes from the upper Sonoran Desert environment into piñon-juniper chaparral. Negotiable by passenger cars (and therefore best on weekdays), the road is bumpy enough to keep the traffic low and slow; it dead-ends at the Barnhardt Trailhead to the Mazatzal Wilderness. Consider combining the ride with a day hike into the spectacular dry-mountain wilderness, or perhaps spending the night at the trailhead, where you'll find several undeveloped campsites with plenty of aromatic juniper and piñon firewood available.

Go south from Payson on State Highway 87, dropping for 10 miles. Immediately after crossing the bridge over Rye Creek, 1 mile

At the Barnhardt Trailhead rocky paths invite exploration by foot

south of the settlement of Rye, turn right onto Forest Road 419 and park.

Pedal up Forest Road 419, climbing toward Barnhardt Trailhead and the imposing Mazatzal Mountains. It may seem quite civilized near the highway, but a sense of remoteness quickly takes over. The grade steepens after 1.5 miles; gaining elevation, you earn long-distance vistas of the surrounding countryside. It's particularly beautiful here along Barnhardt Mesa in the spring, when sparse grass lends a light-green hue to the terrain, prickly pear and hedgehog cacti bloom in living color, and hundreds of tall agave stalks reach for the sky.

At 2.4 temporarily top out; the uphill grade again steepens for a few hundred yards at 3.1 miles. At 4.0, approaching the mountains, the road becomes very rocky. At 5.3 miles you're at the Barnhardt Trailhead and the border of the Mazatzal Wilderness. Here, trails shoot off in three directions, inviting exploration by foot.

Coasting back, enjoy the expansive view of the high chaparral and broad desert basin beyond.

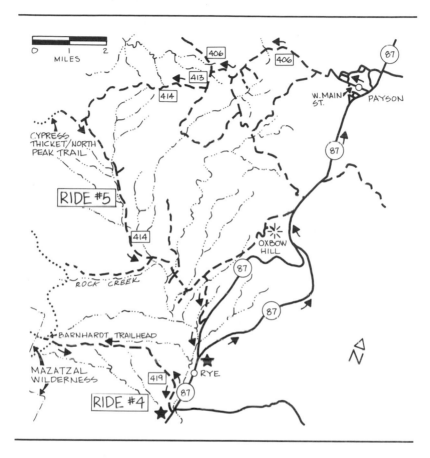

5. Cypress Thicket Loop

Riding surface:	Smooth dirt, pavement
Elevation range:	3,125 to 5,020 feet
Distance:	30.7 miles
Relative difficulty:	Hard
Time to allow:	3 to 5 hours
Best time of year:	March through May; September through November
Supplemental map:	Tonto National Forest visitors map

You can begin this outing in Payson, but the anticlimactic ending will include an unforgettable 8-mile climb along the busy highway back into town. Advisably, drive to Rye and begin there. Or, if you'd prefer to avoid the long, paved uphill altogether, shuttle a second car to Rye, drive to Payson, and pick up the route narrative at mile 10.2. (This scenario creates an easy-rated ride of 20.5 miles.) Another option is to complete the loop in reverse, coasting down the pavement and enjoying the elevation gain on dirt.

Rye, 10 miles south of Payson, is immediately south of where the split north- and southbound lanes of State Highway 87 merge.

Pedal north along State Highway 87; pace yourself for this hard climb into Payson. At 5.8 miles you earn a temporary topping out, but the uphill resumes with a vengeance in 0.5 mile. Look up now and then, wipe the sweat from your eyes, and notice as the elevation rises that the vegetation is changing from that of desert scrub to piñon-juniper; by the time you reach Payson, ponderosa pine forest dominates.

At 8.2 miles is the top of the hill—finally! Along the flatter 2-mile approach to Payson note the distinctive, uniform backdrop of the Mogollon Rim. At 10.2 miles, at the first stop light in town, turn left (south) onto West Main (the local visitors center is at this corner). Begin a gentle downgrade, which endures for the next 3.5 miles.

At 11.4 the road curves left to become South Verde Road; at 11.7 it curves back right and becomes Country Club Drive. At 12.2 miles, while skirting the golf course, the road surface turns to gravel. At 12.4 pass a sign designating your route as Forest Road 406. At 12.9, after crossing a cattle guard and passing the fragrant water-treatment plant, ride through a little stream; pass through it again at 13.3 miles. You've lost a substantial amount of elevation since Payson; here the open valley is surrounded by hills studded with juniper and gambel oak.

At 13.6 miles the creek veers downcanyon to the right; begin up a steep hill. At 14.1 crest the saddle, to be met with a view of the Mazatzal Mountains. Continue on the main road as a series of primitive roads fork left at 14.5, 14.8, and at 15.0 miles, where you begin down. At 15.5 turn left downhill onto Forest Road 413 toward Cypress Thicket, as Forest Road 406 goes right. At 16.1 bottom out in a draw; in 0.25 mile bear right toward Cypress Thicket onto Forest Road 414 (the left-hand road is signed "Forest Protection Road") and resume coasting. Winding, twisting, and rolling down through pleasing piñon-juniper forest for the next few miles, you'll begin to wonder if the downhill ever ends. It does.

Note the occasional stands of Arizona cypress, with their scaly bark. At 20.8 miles, where a road going right is signed "Cypress Thicket/North Peak Trail," continue straight, and down, down, down. At 22.4 pass over a cattle guard; at 23.3 continue straight as another road goes left. During the next mile splash through five water crossings, en route passing a couple of inviting, undeveloped campsites. You've given up enough elevation now that the ground cover includes abundant prickly pear and barrel cacti.

At 25.6 ride through a creek bed; bright red cliffs contrast with the relatively drab landscape. Continue on the main road after crossing the creek bed at 25.6 (at this point another road goes right, following Rock Creek upstream). At 26.5 climb out of the draw, then continue climbing in earnest. In 0.1 mile ride straight ahead as forks go left and right (the one to the right is signed "Dead End"). At 26.8 miles crest the first of two ridges separating you from the highway, and begin down. At 27.3 hook 90 degrees left, as a primitive road goes right, and pedal gradually uphill. At 28.0 curve sharply right (the Oxbow Road, a steep alternate route back to the highway, goes left). At 28.5 bottom out and start up.

Top out again at 29.1, coast for 0.5 mile down to a cattle guard and begin the final approach to the highway. At 30.1 switchback hard left, then turn right onto State Highway 87 at 30.3. At 30.7 miles return to Rye.

6. Ride of the Purple Sage

Riding surface:	Smooth dirt, pavement
Elevation range:	5,341 to 6,384 feet
Distance:	28 miles
Relative difficulty:	Moderate
Time to allow:	3 to 5 hours
Best time of year:	March through November
Supplemental map:	Tonto National Forest visitors map

The following route includes two yo-yo spurs: one up to the Diamond Point Lookout and the other to the Zane Grey Cabin site. The outing can be shortened to 15.4 miles by eliminating the spurs; however, both are recommended. The road to Diamond Point offers one of the easiest "lookout rides" in the West. Vacation homes line portions of the route, so prepare for a bustle of activity in summer, especially on weekends. Things slow down considerably in the spring and autumn. The ride skirts the base of the Mogollon Rim, the 1,000-foot-high cliff running for miles and miles across central Arizona.

From Payson, go 17.5 miles east on State Highway 260 and turn left onto Forest Road 289. Park at the Tonto Creek Campground.

Leave the campground and turn right onto Forest Road 289. Turn right (west) onto State Highway 260 at 0.3 mile. Cross Tonto

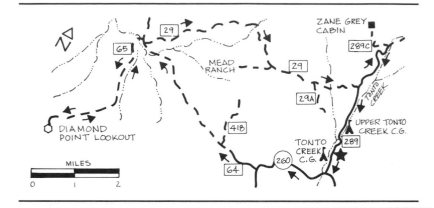

Creek at 0.5 and begin a 1.5-mile uphill. At 0.6 Kohl's Ranch, with store and lodge, is on the right. At 2.2 miles, turn right onto paved Forest Road 64.

The pavement ends at 3.2 and the riding is rolling for the next 1 mile plus. At 4.9 head down a big hill; continue downstream on Forest Road 64 at 6.0 as Forest Road 418 joins on the right. At 6.5 pass the right-hand turn to Forest Road 29 (turn onto it now if you're not interested in riding to Diamond Point); in another 0.1 mile turn left onto Forest Road 65 toward Diamond Point and begin a gradual uphill. At 7.8 the hill steepens slightly, but is still moderately pitched for a lookout access road.

Alternating between steep and gentle pitches for the next 2.5 miles, arrive at the gate to the lookout at 10.0 and the lookout itself at 10.3 miles. Curiously, probably due to greater exposure to the sun, the conditions become more desert-like the higher you get, changing from ponderosa pine forest to a cover of juniper and agave closer to the lookout.

Retrace your tracks back down the fun descent to Forest Road 29, which you turn left onto at 14.1 miles. Hit a steep upgrade at 14.4, topping out at 14.7. Begin up another 0.5-mile-long hill at 15.1; at the top is a good view of Roberts Mesa, directly in front. Continue along a series of dips and rises, passing through a stand of immense oaks and junipers at 17.5 miles. At 18.1 bear left onto the more primitive, red-surfaced road, signed "Tonto Creek 3 miles" (the road you're veering off curves right toward the Mead Ranch private-homes area). Although the nature of the road surface changes, you're still following Forest Road 29.

At 19.5 miles primitive Forest Road 29A goes right; continue straight. At 20.2 miles dip through impressive Big Canyon draw and start a steep and rocky uphill. At 20.8 coast down, crossing a cattle guard in 0.25 mile, and turn left uphill at 21.1 onto paved Forest Road 289, toward the Zane Grey Cabin site (turn right if you don't wish to visit the historic site).

Topping out at 22.5, coast down to 22.8 and turn left onto Forest Road 289C toward the Zane Grey Cabin site. At 23.6 miles arrive at the site (the cabin itself was burned to the ground by a 1990 forest fire). The famous author of classic Westerns such as *Riders of the Purple Sage* built the place in the early 1920s as a hunting retreat and wilderness getaway. Originally from Zanesville, Ohio, Grey graduated from dental school in Pennsylvania, supporting his schooling with a baseball scholarship. Here, beneath the Mogollon Rim, he wrote *Under the Tonto Rim* and other novels.

Head back the way you came, passing at 26.1 miles the point where you turned off Forest Road 29; continue downhill on pavement. At 27.4 pass Upper Tonto Creek Campground and arrive back at Tonto Creek Campground at 28.0 miles.

Zane Grey's hideout, before it burned in a 1990 forest fire

Mogollon Rim

The Mogollon Rim, which spans 200 miles of central Arizona, is an erosional escarpment defining the southern edge of the vast Colorado Plateau. Along its length the cliff averages 1,000 feet from base to top, and the elevation of the rolling terrain behind the Rim ranges from 7,000 to 8,000 feet above sea level. The Rim country provides a haven of timber cover for wildlife, and while riding here you may spot wild turkey and big-game species such as deer, elk, and black bear.

Gazing out over half of Arizona

Winter hits hard on the Rim, but pleasant summer temperatures create cycling conditions that can't be beat in the Grand Canyon State. Be warned—hordes of desert dwellers flock to the Rim for its cool temperatures and shade-providing stands of ponderosa pine, and for its abundance of roads and trails, fishing lakes, and campgrounds. The crowds can be avoided by visiting in spring or autumn, which also offer ideal weather for cycling.

The terrain along the Mogollon Plateau is generally quite flat and uniformly pine-covered—pleasant but not spectacular—and riddled with logging roads to explore. The best access to these by-ways is provided by the Mogollon Rim Road (Forest Road 300), its western end beginning approximately 15 miles north of the town of Pine (see ride 7).

This high-grade gravel road, known today as the General Crook Trail, was built during pioneer days to connect Camp Verde and Fort Apache. A designated National Recreation Trail, it makes a good mountain-bike route during the off-tourist seasons. Hugging the Rim, the road provides glimpses over the edge and into the basins and deserts to the south.

The supplemental map needed for the Mogollon Rim is the Coconino National Forest visitors map, available through the Forest Supervisor's Office, 2323 East Greenlaw Lane, Flagstaff, AZ 86001, (602) 527-7400, or at district offices in Rimrock, Flagstaff, Happy Jack, and Sedona.

7. Milk Ranch Point

Riding surface:	Gravel
Elevation range:	7,000 to 7,440 feet
Distance:	13.6 miles
Relative difficulty:	Easy
Time to allow:	2 to 3 hours
Best time of year:	May through October
Supplemental map:	Coconino National Forest visitors map

This straightforward out-and-back ride leads to the edge of the Mogollon Rim, providing glorious views into the Payson basin and the Mazatzal Wilderness beyond. There's an inviting, undeveloped campsite at the turnaround point—the perfect spot to look out over the desert on a moonlit, coyote-yelping night. Watch for elk and other wildlife on this outing.

From Pine (15 miles northwest of Payson), head northwest on

State Highway 87 as it winds up and onto the Mogollon Rim, then veers northeast, for a total of approximately 15 miles. Park on the right, at the road signed "Knoll Lake/Rim Road." (From Flagstaff, the junction is about 65 miles south on Forest Road 3 and State Highway 87.)

Pedal south on Forest Road 218A toward Rim Road. At 0.1 mile Rim Road (Forest Road 300) goes left; continue straight on Forest Road 218A. (Note: from this point it's a short side-trip on Forest Road 300 to the Baker Butte lookout; at 8,200 feet, it occupies the highest point along the Mogollon Rim.) At 1.6 curve right onto Forest Road 218; Forest Road 218A ends. Continue along alternating stretches of up and down.

At 2.8, at a cattle-loading chute and an undeveloped campsite, good views over the Rim can be obtained by walking a few hundred feet to the left of the road. Pass by a small reservoir at 3.6; continue up and down. The forest cover is primarily of ponderosa pine, with a juniper and oak understory. You'll recognize immediately the occasional alligator juniper, and why it's called that. The odd-looking squirrels scampering about are known as Abert's squirrels, a close relative of the

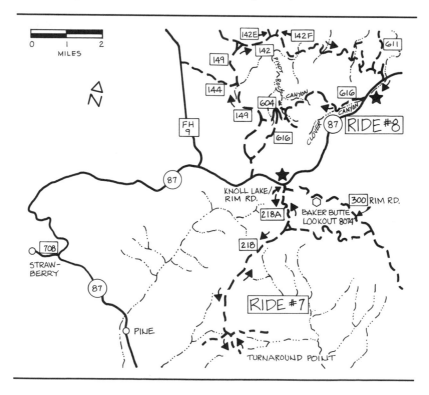

Kaibab squirrel, found living only along the North Rim of the Grand Canyon.

At 5.4 miles Forest Road 218 ends where primitive roads go right and left; follow the left fork. Go up for 0.1 mile to where the road splits again, and this time choose the right fork. Coast downhill through timber to 6.8 and the road's end at the Rim's edge. Gaze out over half of Arizona.

Returning, you have a steep uphill for 1.5 miles, and then a relatively easy ride back to the beginning point, reached at 13.6.

8. Coconino Roller Coaster

Riding surface:	Gravel, pavement
Elevation range:	6,646 to 7,117 feet
Distance:	14.5 miles
Relative difficulty:	Moderate
Time to allow:	2 to 3 hours
Best time of year:	May through October
Supplemental map:	Coconino National Forest visitors map

Dipping and climbing through a series of oak-filled draws in an uncharacteristically hilly part of the Mogollon Plateau, this route at one point brushes up against the West Clear Creek Wilderness Area. You'll pass numerous undeveloped campsites and several inviting spur roads following the ridges trending to the north of Forest Road 142. The entire loop is negotiable by passenger cars *and* log trucks, so check with Coconino National Forest personnel to find if nearby cutting operations are underway. The ride is best taken on weekdays in summer, any day in spring and fall.

Park at the junction of State Highway 87 and Forest Road 616, 3.7 miles northeast of Forest Road 218A, where the Milk Ranch Point ride begins (see ride 7).

Pedal southwest on Forest Road 616, following the sign directing you to "Pivot Rock Canyon 4/Wildcat Springs 6." Note the fossil shells embedded in limestone outcrops along the right. This high-grade, ditched-and-crowned road pokes into Clover Canyon as low, pine-covered ridges rise to the sides. At 0.9 mile curve through a drainage, skirting a stand of large quaking aspen on the left.

Go up and down for the next couple of miles, passing several gated-shut spur roads. At 2.9 spin through an open ponderosa pine park, followed by a 0.5-mile downhill. At 3.4 round a corner in Pivot Rock Canyon; primitive roads going both left and right invite off-route sniffing around. After climbing out of the canyon, at 3.8 miles bear right onto Forest Road 604, as Forest Road 616 curves left.

Continue up and down; at 4.6 miles head straight (right) onto Forest Road 149, which is curving left at this point. Hit the canyon bottom at 6.1, where exploration roads go left and right. Forest Road 144 goes left as you continue straight uphill on Forest Road 149. At 7.4 miles bear right at the Y onto Forest Road 142.

Continue straight at 8.4 where Forest Road 142E goes left (leading north to a wilderness overlook) and again as Forest Road 142F goes left at 8.6. At 9.6 miles you'll find some pleasant, undeveloped campsites along the creek. Splash through the creek at 9.7 and begin a mile-long uphill, skirting the wilderness area. The road continues to dip through canyon and rise over ridge.

At 13.0 miles continue straight on Forest Road 142 as Forest Road 611 goes left. At 13.6 cross a cattle guard and turn right at the T toward State Highway 87 (left heads toward Clover Springs). At 14.2 turn right onto State Highway 87 and return to the beginning point at 14.5 miles.

9. Oak Hill Loop

Riding surface:	Smooth to rock-embedded dirt road, pavement
Elevation range:	5,800 to 6,325 feet
Distance:	16.1 miles
Relative difficulty:	Moderate
Time to allow:	2 to 3 hours
Best time of year:	March through November
Supplemental map:	Coconino National Forest visitors map

This outing leads through the pleasant, transitional oak-piñon chaparral lying between the high Mogollon Rim and the Verde River Valley below. Be certain your odometer is working, for there are several opportunities to go wrong. A good base camp is the Clear Creek Campground, 11 miles west of the starting point. After the ride, flip a coin and have the loser drive back down to the campground while the others coast down the tremendous, paved Devils Windpipe downhill, which loses more than 2,000 feet of elevation in 12 miles.

From Camp Verde, proceed east for 17 miles on Forest Highway 9; park at the unsigned road going north (it's 2.8 miles east of a historical marker).

Spin up the cinder-covered road and turn right in 0.2 mile. Hit a

Oak Hill

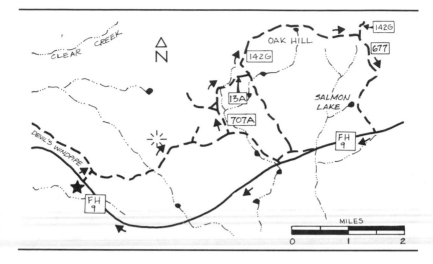

stretch of rocks at 0.6 as you roll through a beautiful grassland punctuated with piñon and juniper stands. Top out at 1.1, viewing ahead
the canyon of Clear Creek and the tips of the distant San Francisco
Peaks.

At 2.5 cross a dry wash and turn right at the fork (the left fork
skirts to the left of a cattle pond), passing through a fenceline at 2.6. At
2.9 miles go through a gate where, at 3.0, a path comes in from the
left—bear straight ahead at this point. At the fork at 3.3 miles, turn left
onto unsigned Forest Road 707A. (Note: for a shorter outing, turn
right here, arriving back at the highway at 4.4, then again turn right
and return to the beginning point at 8.7.)

Go right at the Y at 3.8 miles and continue straight uphill as another road joins from the left at 3.9. At 4.8 turn right onto the curving
Forest Road 13A as the track you're on ends. At 5.1 miles turn left onto
142G (right goes to "Macks #2" spring and back to the highway).
At 6.1 head up on the main path rather than down the more primitive
one. At 6.4, after a steep pitch, pass through a gate and arrive at *the*
lunch spot: here, huge pines surround a pond, and Oak Hill rises ahead
on the left.

At 6.5 skirt to the left of a small dam, then climb steeply to 6.7
and crest Oak Hill. Wind lazily down the ridgeline to 7.9, and turn
right at the T onto Forest Road 677, where Forest Road 142G goes
left. At the saddle at 8.6 pass through a gap in an electric-fence and start
down. Hit bottom at 9.1 with a big, red quarry ahead; at 9.4 Salmon
Lake is on the right.

Family fun in Oak Creek Canyon

At 9.7, with a pleasant, primitive campsite on the right, begin climbing. Top out at 10.0 and turn right onto the paved shoulder of Forest Highway 9. Go down for a mile, crossing Tin Can Draw, then spin along a level stretch for a couple of miles. Climb from 13.4 to 15.0, and start down in earnest. (Note: this is the beginning of the Devils Windpipe downhill, which continues to the Clear Creek crossing, 12 miles distant.) Arrive back at the beginning point at 16.1 miles. Some fun, huh?

Sedona–Jerome

The redrock country surrounding posh Sedona includes some of the most beautiful scenery in Arizona. Oak Creek Canyon—with its towering spires, natural waterslides, and famous fall colors—at its bottom is as far as 3,000 feet below the looming Mogollon Rim. While pedaling in the Sedona area, don't be surprised to find yourself expecting at any time to meet the Lone Ranger or John Wayne riding around the next bend, for the redrock monoliths look like those featured in every Western ever made. Indeed, hundreds of movies have been filmed in the area.

Appropriately, much of the land surrounding Sedona is designated wilderness. But there are gaps and corridors of nonwilderness lands that you can penetrate on fat tires, and gain access to the hiking trailheads.

Jerome, 25 miles southwest of Sedona, is perched precariously on the side of Cleopatra Hill, high above the Verde River Valley. The boutiqued and artist-inhabited old "Billion Dollar Copper Camp," with a onetime population of 15,000, is now a major tourist attraction. There may no longer be millions to be made here digging for minerals, but still awaiting discovery is a wealth of top-notch mountain-biking routes. Simply head above town, to the slopes of Mingus Mountain, and *eureka!*

The supplemental map needed for the Sedona area is the Coconino National Forest visitors map, available through the Forest Supervisor's Office, 2323 East Greenlaw Lane, Flagstaff, AZ 86001, (602) 527-7400, and at district offices in Rimrock, Happy Jack, and Sedona. For the Jerome vicinity pick up the Prescott National Forest visitors map, available through the Forest Supervisor's Office, 344 South Cortez Street, Prescott, AZ 86301, (602) 445-1762, and at district offices in Chino Valley, Prescott, and Camp Verde.

10. Red Rock Ramble

Riding surface:	Sand and dirt, sandstone outcrops
Elevation range:	4,590 to 4,800 feet
Distance:	9 miles
Relative difficulty:	Easy
Time to allow:	2 to 3 hours
Best time of year:	March through May; September through November
Supplemental map:	Coconino National Forest visitors map

Poking into a gap in the south side of the Secret Mountain Wilderness, this route provides access to several pleasant, undeveloped campsites and to trailheads for hikes into magic spots like Secret Canyon, H S Canyon, and Vultee Arch. The road, open to cars, is rough enough that typically it's traveled only by those with four-wheel-drive vehicles. Although this is a popular route for local jeep-tour companies, by getting an early start you'll avoid encountering many four-wheelers. Juniper, piñon and prickly pear cactus decorate the intensely red canyons and low ridges you will ride through and across.

From the junction of State Highway 179 and U.S. Highway 89A in Sedona, go 3.3 miles west on U.S. Highway 89 and turn north onto Forest Road 152C. Continue up Forest Road 152C for 2 miles, and park at the junction with Dry Creek Road/Forest Road 152. (Note: beginning the ride at the junction of U.S. Highway 89 and Forest Road 152C will add 4 pleasant and rolling, paved miles to the ride.)

Climb north on Dry Creek Road/Forest Road 152 for 0.2 mile,

then descend through a slickrock drainage. The next mile is predominantly downhill, over a rocky and sandy road surface. At 1.3 miles Forest Road 910 goes left into an undeveloped camping spot. In another 0.1 mile Forest Road 915/Trail 120 heads right toward Devils Bridge. (It's about 1 mile round-trip to the sandstone arch, approximately half of which can be ridden along a primitive road. The arch itself, within the Secret Mountain Wilderness, must be approached on foot.)

Zip down through a slickrock draw at 1.9; at 2.1 a dirt track accesses some primitive campsites. Forest Road 913 goes right at 2.3; atop a hill at 2.4 miles Trail 119 goes right toward Brins Mesa, entering the wilderness in 0.25 mile. At 2.5, Forest Road 979 goes right, and at 3.5 miles Trail 121 heads left into Secret Canyon. Negotiate a stretch of sand-covered road, and at 4.5 miles arrive at the wilderness boundary and road's end. It's a 2-mile hike to the east to Vultee Arch; another trail runs north into Bear Sign Canyon.

After hiking around and enjoying the sunshine and redrock splendor, backtrack to your point of origin, reached at 9.0 miles.

The Red Rock Ramble road

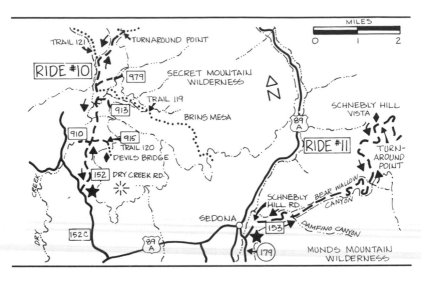

11. Damfino Up from Down

Riding surface: Smooth dirt
Elevation range: 4,200 to 5,980 feet
Distance: 13 miles
Relative difficulty: Moderate
Time to allow: 2 to 3 hours
Best time of year: March through June; September through
                       November
Supplemental map: Coconino National Forest visitors map

This up-once, down-once ride includes panoramic views into Oak Creek Canyon and the distant Verde River Valley, lying to the southwest. The all-weather road is passenger-car graded and numerous tourists motor up on weekends, so weekdays are your best bet. One suggested itinerary is to climb the hill in the evening and set up camp, watching the sun set over the redrock country, and then coast out at sunrise.

En route to the destination of Schnebly Hill Vista, you ascend through a cross-section of the area's brilliantly colored geologic formations, including the intensely red Schnebly Hill Formation and, atop that, the cliff-forming, dust-white Coconino Sandstone.

In the late 1800s, settlers longing for a negotiable route connecting the Verde River Valley and Flagstaff began hand-building a roadbed along the tortuous terrain you'll be traversing. By 1902 horses

Bear Wallow Canyon

and wagons could at last manage their way up and onto the Mogollon Rim. For more than a decade thereafter, this hand-built path served as the main route going north, until the road through Oak Creek Canyon was pieced together. First known as the Verde Cutoff, then Munds Road, Schnebly Hill Road derives its name from a guest house operated by the D. E. Schnebly family that was located near today's Tlaquepaque arts plaza.

From the junction of State Highway 179 and U.S. Highway 89A in Sedona, go 0.4 mile south on State Highway 179 toward the town of Oak Creek. Park at the turnoff to Schnebly Hill Road.

Head east on paved Schnebly Hill Road; at 0.3 mile the pavement ends. Piercing Bear Wallow Canyon, the road skirts the northern border of the Munds Mountain Wilderness Area. At 0.6, just past a cattleguard crossing, a sign designates the road as Forest Road 153. The road, wide and hard, takes you into a cavernous redrock basin.

At 1.4 round the toe of a ridge, then curve left through the sandy bottom of Damfino Creek. Following a short downhill, resume climbing at 2.0, passing beneath a big rock face at 3.0 miles. Switchback hard left at 3.2, then again at 4.1. At 5.1 miles you're at the first of several mandatory stop-and-be-awed viewpoints. In another 0.25 mile, pass through a gap in the rock, exiting Bear Wallow Canyon, and entering an entirely different viewing perspective.

Curve left through a draw at 6.1 and arrive at the Schnebly Hill Vista at 6.5 miles. The road continues east for 6 miles to the Little Antelope Interchange on Interstate 17; unless you've arranged for a shuttle or are on a self-supported longer tour, do a "180" and coast back. But not before soaking up the inspiring views into Oak Creek Canyon and beyond.

12. Mingus Mountain

Riding surface:	Rocky jeep road and pavement
Elevation range:	5,800 to 6,720 feet
Distance:	7.9 miles
Relative difficulty:	Moderate
Time to allow:	2 to 3 hours
Best time of year:	April through November
Supplemental map:	Prescott National Forest visitors map

Out of the Verde River Valley you climb, high above Tuzigoot National Monument, home to a band of the prehistoric Sinagua ("without water") Indians. Up, up, through the revived ghost town of Jerome, and still up, into ponderosa pine forest. Circling a big basin high in the Black Hills of the Prescott National Forest, this route skirts the southern edge of the Woodchute Wilderness Area.

The view from Mingus Mountain Loop

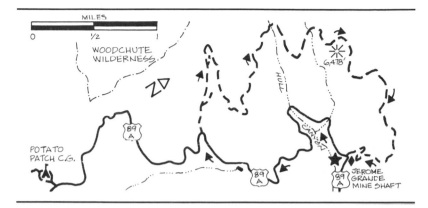

The route includes a potentially busy stretch of U.S. Highway 89A; traffic should be minimal during early morning. Potato Patch Campground, a good base camp, is about 5 miles above the ride's beginning point.

From the severely slanting town of Jerome, continue up U.S. Highway 89A for 2.2 miles and park at the right-hand pullout, where a rough road comes down steeply from above.

Start by fighting gravity on U.S. Highway 89A, gaining elevation for nearly 2 miles along the winding road. At 1.8 round a right-hand curve and begin down. At 2.2 miles pass the Prescott National Forest sign and head up; at 2.6 miles turn right onto a dirt path as the highway curves left.

After passing through the gate in a fenceline, ascend along the steep and rough path, its smooth, pine-needle-covered surface interrupted by some very rocky stretches. At 2.9, fork left uphill. Bear left again at 3.2 miles, then drop down through the drainage bottom. Resume climbing at 3.6, topping out at 3.8 on a ridge offering grand views of the Verde River Valley and the redrock country to the north.

At 4.0, following a badly eroded stretch of downhill, bear left into the big basin. Ride a level contour for the next couple of miles, with only a few gentle ups and downs. At 4.9 cross through a drainage and curve right. At 5.2 miles round the ridge, noticing the water catch-pool (for wildlife) just to the right. At 5.7 is a U.S. Geological Survey brass cap, marking the 6,478-foot elevation. At 6.3 miles round the ridge and head up into a big draw.

At 6.9 miles begin the radical and rocky plunge down to the highway. At 7.7 switchback right, noting the *deep*, fenced-off Jerome Grande Mine Shaft on the left. At 7.9 miles pass through the gate and back to the beginning point.

Spring riding in Flagstaff's Dry Hills Trail System

Flagstaff–Grand Canyon

When in Flagstaff, elevation 7,000 feet, you may decide you've unknowingly been whisked out of Arizona and a thousand miles north. The feel of the town is much closer to that of Bend, Oregon, or Bozeman, Montana, than to Phoenix or Tucson. Ponderosa pines blanket the rolling countryside surrounding the city, and the San Francisco Peaks, reaching 12,670 feet at Humphreys Peak, attract skiers during their long, white season. Like many college towns, Flagstaff—home to Northern Arizona State University—is an athletic- and outdoor-minded community. You'll meet more mountain bikers here than anywhere else in Arizona.

Known as the City of Seven Wonders, within 90 minutes' driving time of town are the San Francisco Peaks, Meteor Crater and the Astronauts Hall of Fame, Sunset Crater National Monument (an extinct volcano), Walnut Canyon National Monument (cliff dwellings), Wapatki National Monument (a three-story Indian ruin), Oak Creek

Canyon, and—perhaps the most wonderful in the entire United States—the Grand Canyon.

The supplemental map needed for the Flagstaff area is the Coconino National Forest visitors map, available through the Forest Supervisor's Office, 2323 East Greenlaw Lane, Flagstaff, AZ 86001, (602) 527-7400, and at district offices in Rimrock, Happy Jack, and Sedona. Also available at local outfitting stores and at the Forest Service offices is a sketch map of the Mount Elden-Dry Lake Hills Trail System. The map includes ride 13 and depicts several other trails.

For the Grand Canyon vicinity you need the south half Kaibab National Forest visitors map, available through the Forest Supervisor's Office, 800 South Sixth Street, Williams, AZ 86046, (602) 635-2681, and at district offices in Fredonia and Tusayan. At the visitors center, you can purchase an excellent waterproof topo map of the park that includes the Cape Solitude Getaway route, ride 14.

13. Mount Elden Lookout Loop

Riding surface:	Trail, gravel road
Elevation range:	7,200 to 9,299 feet
Distance:	16.1 miles
Relative difficulty:	Hard
Time to allow:	3 to 5 hours
Best time of year:	May through October
Supplemental map:	Coconino National Forest visitors map, Mount Elden-Dry Hills Trail System map

For a couple of reasons, this ride has you gaining elevation on trails, and losing it on a road. First, the trail system is used by hikers and equestrians, so chances are you'll be going slowly (uphill) if and when you encounter other users. Second, the trail portions of the route are more aesthetically pleasing than the section along road. By heading uphill on the trails you'll spend relatively more time on them, while traveling slowly enough to appreciate your surroundings.

Getting to this ride you'll pass by the Museum of Northern Arizona. Well worth a visit, it includes presentations on geology, biology, and paleontology, and outstanding displays on the archaeology of the Colorado Plateau. The museum includes over a million archaeological and ethnological artifacts. A regularly changing exhibit features the present-day art of the Hopi, Navajo, Zuni, and other regional Indian tribes. A visit to the museum will enrich your visit to the Four Corners

Region by familiarizing you with its complex natural and cultural aspects.

From Flagstaff, go northwest on U.S. Highway 180. Just beyond the Museum of Northern Arizona, turn right onto Schultz Pass Road and follow the pavement as it curves left in 0.25 mile. In another 0.25 mile, pass through a gate and turn right downhill into the parking area. (Note: you can park and begin at the museum, adding a total of 1.2 miles to the ride.)

From the parking area, ride north up the ponderosa-shaded trail. At 0.6 continue bearing right along the trail, heading upstream. At 0.8 mile pedal onto the signed Schultz Creek Trail. The trail, the only one in the Mount Elden system open to motorcycles, was built by the Coconino Motorcycle Trail Riders in the 1970s. Negotiate a short, technical rocky section before climbing above the creek.

At 1.2, following a tricky draw crossing, a double-track path merges with the trail. At 2.7 cross to the left side of the creek, to be greeted with a tough climb. Note that the forest is becoming more diversified, with aspen and fir intermingling with ponderosa pine. At 3.6 cross Forest Road 789, passing over a motorcycle barricade, and ride straight onto the trail posted as open to bicycles but closed to motorcycles. In 0.1 mile, veer right away from Schultz Pass Road, heading up a draw.

At 4.0 enter a broad meadow with a signed trailhead; here you're rewarded with open views, to the left, of the Kachina Peaks Wilderness.

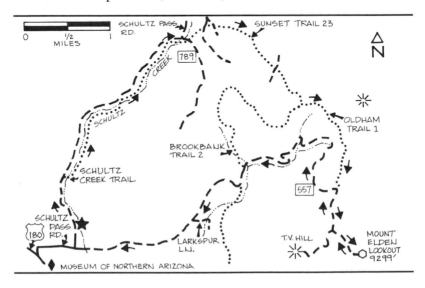

Cross the road and continue straight along the trail for about 100 yards, toward a second trailhead sign. At 4.1 cross a second road and head toward yet another trailhead sign, this one situated in a large parking area. Ride onto Sunset Trail 23, which offers smooth coasting to 4.6, where it heads up a steep draw through a forest of gigantic aspen and fir.

At 5.3 miles cross over a road and continue up the trail, very steep in places. At 5.8 top out on a ridge. Go down to 6.0, and bear left downhill toward Oldham Trail 1 (Brookbank Trail 2 goes right).

At 6.4 miles, in a grassy ponderosa pine park, start up a steep and occasionally rocky slope. At 6.9 arrive at a saddle jumbled with rhyolite boulders; at 7.1 top out on the ridgeline leading up to the lookout tower. Sit down, catch your breath, and take in the fabulous views, across the old burn, of the Flagstaff basin and numerous volcanic cinder cones beyond. Continue alternately walking and riding along the sometimes precarious, loose-dirt trail.

At 7.5 miles turn right toward Brookbank Trail 2, then turn left onto the gravel road in about 150 yards. At 8.1 bear left at the fork in the road, dropping down into a saddle where you begin your final, steep, 0.5-mile approach to the lookout. At 8.8 arrive at the lookout, and the site of an assortment of other-worldly-looking communications and electronics equipment. This is the spot for lunch.

Zip back down to the saddle, crawl back up to the TV Hill junction at 9.4, and begin a long downhill. At 10.0 continue straight past the point where you turned onto this road (at mile 7.6). Switchback left at 12.1, then right. At 12.8 Brookbank Trail 2 joins on the right and drops off to the left at 13.0. At 14.3 miles Larkspur Lane goes left; continue straight through a rural residential area as the road levels off.

At 15.7 miles turn right. Pass through the gate at 15.9, and turn right at 16.1 miles, returning to the parking area.

14. Cape Solitude Getaway

Riding surface:	Smooth to very rocky jeep road
Elevation range:	5,820 to 6,910 feet
Distance:	30 miles
Relative difficulty:	Hard
Time to allow:	6 to 10 hours
Best time of year:	April through May; September through November
Supplemental map:	South half Kaibab National Forest visitors map; Grand Canyon National Park topographic map

This ride, as its name suggests, will leave you feeling quite alone in the world. You'll find it difficult to believe that you're in Grand Canyon National Park, among the world's most popular attractions, with 4 million visitors each year. You'll earn perspectives of the canyon gained by few. Though views of the deep canyon are fleeting, those few stolen glimpses into the improbable depths will surprise and astound.

It's a hefty and rocky ride to Cape Solitude. Elevation is lost in getting there, so the return ride seems even longer. Carry *plenty* of water—you definitely will not want to hike down to the river to fill water bottles. Consider spending the night at the turnaround point; to do so on the night of a full moon would be a magical experience. (Note: if you do plan to camp, you must first acquire a backcountry permit from the park headquarters.)

From Desert View, 25 miles east of Grand Canyon Village, go 3 miles south toward the East Entrance. Immediately before exiting the park, turn left and park at the ranger's trailer. Give a knock and let the ranger on duty know what you're up to.

Roll gradually downhill along the road leading northeast from the ranger's trailer. At 0.4 mile bear straight as another fork heads right. You're riding among piñon and juniper, typical forest cover on the Grand Canyon's South Rim. At 1.0 the road becomes noticeably rockier as it begins dropping off the Kaibab Monocline.

At 1.2, at a right-hand switchback, are the first sweeping views of the Grand Canyon and its sculptor, the Colorado River. Two more switchbacks immediately follow. Still heading down at 2.1, note the Desert View Watch Tower on the rim to your left. The watchtower, a beacon of civilization seen by those floating the Colorado River through the wilderness depths of the Grand Canyon, was designed by

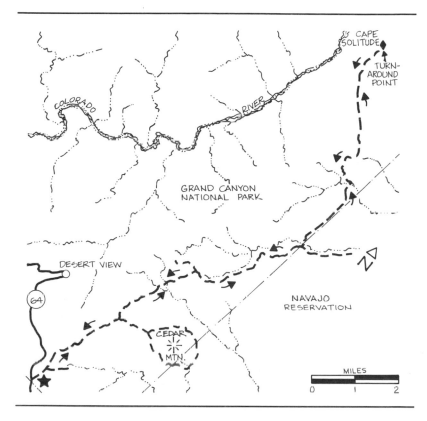

renowned architect Mary Jane Colter. Also the designer of the South Rim's Hopi House and of Phantom Ranch, Colter strove to echo a Native American motif in her stylized rockwork designs.

At 2.8 miles bear left at the fork, away from distinctive Cedar Mountain. Note that as the piñon and juniper become less abundant, sagebrush predominates as the ground cover. Dip through a series of three draws then, at 3.3 miles, begin coasting downdrainage. After a steep walk at 4.1, top out at 4.4. Coast down; Straight Canyon joins on the right. You're out of the timber altogether now.

Start up at 4.7 and top out at 4.9, forking right on the main track. This ridgetop provides good views over the Painted Desert, to Cedar Mountain on the right, and of the watchtower behind. Round the bend and head down at 5.2; the deep gash in the stark terrain ahead is that created by the Little Colorado River, excavating the way to its confluence with the Colorado.

The Grand Canyon

Ride downridge to 6.5, pedal up a short hill, and then continue down. At 8.3 miles, at the bottom of a long downhill, cross onto the Navajo Reservation, closing the gate behind you. At 8.4 fork left, crossing back into Grand Canyon National Park (again, close the gate). At 5,820 feet, the fork is the low point of the ride; you've given up 1,100 feet of elevation since beginning.

After climbing out of the draw, the road flattens and straightens. At 10.0 cross through the drainage; cross it five more times during the next mile. From the top of a steep and rocky pitch at 11.0 miles, it's relatively flat and smooth the rest of the way.

Pass by an old corral site on the left at 12.0. At 13.8 you hit the canyon's rim on the left and continue skirting it to the turnaround point, at 15.0. In your solitude you're gazing *way down* on the often turquoise-colored Little Colorado River as it flows into the just-as-often dark and murky waters of the big Colorado. Go ahead, feel special, for this sight is seen by few who visit Grand Canyon National Park.

Other Rides in Arizona

If you've enjoyed what rolled beneath your tires in Arizona, there's a lot more where that came from.

Kaibab National Forest. South of the Grand Canyon, miles of access roads crisscross the Tusayan Ranger District of the Kaibab National Forest. The terrain is relatively tame, offering easy to moderate riding conditions through piñon-juniper and ponderosa pine transition forests.

Hundreds of miles of gravel and dirt roads also traverse the higher, drainage-bisected, mixed-conifer country of the North Kaibab Ranger District. Some of these roads continue south into Grand Canyon National Park, providing views from the North Rim into the improbable canyon depths. (Note: the north and south rims of the canyon, a mere 10 miles apart as the raven flies, require 215 miles of driving to get from one to the other.)

In the North Kaibab, you'll spot the odd-looking, pointy eared Kaibab squirrel. He's distinguishable from his cousin the Abert's squirrel, common along the Mogollon Rim and the South Rim of the Grand Canyon, by his white tail and dark body. The two squirrels represent a textbook example of the divergent evolution that can occur when animal populations are geographically separated, as, in this case, by a mile-deep canyon.

Forest personnel at the Williams District of the Kaibab National Forest have established a mountain-bike route along portions of deteriorating, historic U.S. Highway 66. Dubbed "Put Your Kickstand on Route 66" (no fooling!), the two loops included are easily accessible from Interstate 40, just west of Williams.

Arizona–Utah border. Some extremely remote riding opportunities are found just south of the Arizona–Utah border. These include routes in the Antelope Valley, north of the Grand Canyon; the Shivwits Plateau, in Lake Mead National Recreation Area; the Mount Trumbull and Mount Logan areas, between Lake Mead National Recreation Area and Grand Canyon National Park; and the House Rock Valley, between the Paria Canyon-Vermillion Cliffs and Saddle Mountain wilderness areas. Also recommended are portions of the under-development Arizona Trail. For information, contact the Arizona Strip District Office of the Bureau of Land Management, 390 North 3050 East, St. George, UT 84770.

Sedona area. When in the Sedona area, consider following Forest Road 216, just southwest of town, as it loops around Schuerman Mountain. The ride provides access to a short side-trip to Red Rock Crossing and looming Cathedral Butte, unfolding a panorama seen in dozens of classic Westerns. Also try out some of the roads to the west of Red Rock Ramble (ride 10), such as Forest Road 152C, Forest Road 525, and Forest Road 795, which leads to Red Canyon and a trailhead for the short hike to the Palatki prehistoric Sinagua Indian ruins.

Show Low–Springerville–Alpine area. The Mogollon Rim continues eastward across central Arizona from the Strawberry-Pine vicinity. Where it approaches the New Mexico border, in the Show Low-Springerville-Alpine vicinity, an abundance of routes awaits discovery. For guidance, pick up the Apache-Sitgreaves National Forest visitors map, available through the Forest Supervisor's Office, P.O. Box 640, Springerville, AZ 85938, (602) 333-4301, and at district offices in Alpine, Clifton, Winslow, Overgaard, and Lakeside.

Wupatki National Monument. In Wupatki National Monument, 25 miles north of Flagstaff, the administrative "river road" traverses the 7.5 miles separating the visitor center from the Little Colorado River. A pleasant 15-mile round trip, it provides a glimpse of a more subdued Little Colorado than the raging river you saw if you pedaled to Cape Solitude (ride 14).

Tonto National Forest. To the south, in the Tonto National Forest, a couple of difficult rides suggested by Mesa Ranger District personnel include a loop using Forest Roads 201 and 201A, beginning about 55 miles north of Mesa on State Highway 87 (this ride is *tough*). The second loop, beginning just west of Superior, Arizona, follows Forest Roads 252, 172, 172A, 650, 8, and 357.

In the Tonto Basin Ranger District—north of the Pig City Loop (ride 2)—two possible outings include: Forest Road 60 (A-Cross Road), a low-elevation spin through Sonoran Desert vegetation, that offers secluded camping spots along Roosevelt Lake, and Forest Road 71 (Green Back Valley Road), heading east from the settlement of Punkin Center.

2
COLORADO

Southwest Colorado encompasses more than its share of North America's most spectacular mountain scenery. Like skiing, hiking, climbing, jeeping, and other gravity-defying and -dependent sports, the popularity of mountain biking has boomed here. Both Crested Butte and the Durango-Purgatory area are established world-class fat-tire venues, and other spots less heralded rival what those two destinations have to dish out. More difficult than choosing what routes to explore is deciding which *not* to visit, for one could spend a lifetime poking around the mountains and canyons of Colorado's southwestern quadrant, and still leave potential routes unpedaled.

A mountain-bike polo match, Crested Butte

Grand Junction

Grand Junction is situated at the confluence of the Gunnison and Colorado rivers, at the relatively low elevation—for Colorado—of 4,600 feet. A recreational hotbed, the community enjoys very warm summers and mild winters, with high-mountain skiing just 35 miles from town, on the slopes of the Grand Mesa.

Grand Junction enthusiastically overbuilt during the energy-boom 1970s; the subsequent bust left the town with a glut of motels and other services. Taking aim at becoming a tourist destination and filling the spare rooms, Grand Junction recently proclaimed itself the "World Dinosaur Capital." Now the Museum of Western Colorado offers opportunities for visitors to take part in several nearby dinosaur digs, and downtown's Main Street, dubbed "Dinosaur Valley," is home to a half-dozen life-like, animated giant lizards. During the annual Dinosaur Days, festival-goers can take part in social and recreational dino-activities such as the Dinosaur Ball, Supersaurus Slow Pitch, and the T-Rex Tee Off.

There's a wide spectrum of mountain-bike opportunities available in the countryside surrounding Grand Junction. Of the two following rides, the first traverses high desert, and the second the much higher Grand Mesa. Grand Junction is also the northern gateway to the Uncompahgre Plateau, a massive, uplifted tableland, about which an entire mountain-bike guide has been written (see Appendix A). And just west of town is the eastern terminus of Kokopelli's Trail, a mountain-bike route spanning 128 miles between that point and Moab, Utah.

The supplemental map needed for ride 15 can be obtained through the Grand Junction BLM Resource Area, 764 Horizon Drive, Grand Junction, CO 81506, (303) 243-6552. For the Lands End Loop, pick up the Grand Mesa National Forest visitors map, available through the Forest Supervisor's Office, 2250 Highway 50, Delta, CO 81416, (303) 874-7691, and at district offices in Collbran and Grand Junction.

15. Bedrock Bash

Riding surface:	Dirt road with some sandy and rocky stretches
Elevation range:	5,860 to 7,045 feet
Distance:	22 miles
Relative difficulty:	Moderate
Time to allow:	3 to 5 hours
Best time of year:	March through May; September through November
Supplemental map:	Grand Junction BLM Resource Area map

On the ancient landscape in and around scenic Colorado National Monument, past home to several species of dinosaurs, it's easy to picture Fred Flintstone and Barney Rubble rolling along on fat-rock-tire mountain bikes, faithful Dino running alongside, and Fred "Yaaba-daaba-dooing" as they rocket down the hills with feet dragging to slow their speed.

The monument's vertical-walled sandstone canyons mark the northernmost extension of the Uncompahgre Plateau; Wingate sandstone forms the canyon walls and the rims are composed of Kayenta sandstone. Long before the Uncompahgre Plateau was uplifted—when the region was flat and swampy—was when the dinosaurs roamed. Only after the continents split and deserts formed did the sandstone plateaus rise, carrying with them bones of the ancient lizards.

Beginning at the western edge of the national monument (which has a campground that makes an ideal base camp), the ride follows the Black Ridge Hunter Access Road. The turnaround point is the trailhead to Rattlesnake Canyon; following the trail on foot for a couple of miles will lead you down along the rim of the canyon. Formed in the

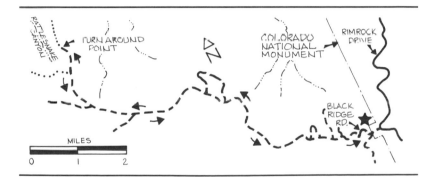

Entrada sandstone formation, the number of natural arches concentrated here is second in the world only to Utah's Arches National Monument, not far to the west.

Remember: going out you lose elevation, so the return trip will take substantially longer. Some ideal undeveloped campsites await at the turnaround point; consider making this an overnighter. The road's expansive soils make bicycle travel impractical during rainy periods, and the millions of black gnats found in the early summer make stopping to fix a flat a miserable proposition.

From the east entrance of Colorado National Monument, 3 miles west of Grand Junction on Monument Road, wind upcanyon along Rimrock Drive. At 11.3 miles from the entrance, turn left onto gravel toward Glade Park, cross a cattle guard, and, in about 100 yards, turn right onto the BLM-signed Black Ridge Road and park.

Begin climbing on the primitive road into a sage- and juniper-filled canyon. At 0.8 mile bear sharply right through a draw, then switchback left; three more switchbacks follow. At 1.4 miles follow the public-access arrow to the right. At 1.8 bear left, away from the road leading toward the radio tower above on a knob; cross over the ridge and, at 1.9, follow the public-access arrow straight. (The path going right leads into the Black Ridge Wilderness Study Area.)

Follow the arrow left at 2.2 miles. At 4.0 miles crest a high point and begin coasting down a rocky slope. At 4.6 pass through an old fenceline and start winding up the scrubby slope. The road levels off at 5.0 miles, providing big views of the Colorado River basin and its desert mountain backdrop. Curve at 5.4, following the public-access arrow; follow another arrow straight at 6.6 miles.

At 8.6—following a series of four fun whoop-de-doo dips and rises—turn right following the arrow and descend along a stretch of rough stuff. At 9.4 miles follow the arrow right, toward the end of the visible point of land. Proceeding through occasional sandy stretches, look down to the left: here and there you'll spot an arch along the canyon rim. At 11.0 is the trailhead and turnaround point. Backtrack to the beginning point, regained at 22.0 miles.

Lands End Road offers one of the all-time great downhills

16. Lands End Loop

Riding surface:	Smooth gravel and rutted dirt road
Elevation range:	9,770 to 10,648 feet
Distance:	29.1 miles
Relative difficulty:	Moderate
Time to allow:	3 to 5 hours
Best time of year:	July through September
Supplemental map:	Grand Mesa National Forest visitors map

The Grand Mesa, rising a mile above the Grand Valley, was known to the Ute Indians as Thigunawat, or "home of departed spirits." Millions of years ago, through a series of eruptions, a lake bottom was covered with oozing lava flows. This volcanic rock, 200 to 400 feet thick, was responsible for creating the Grand Mesa by protecting its underlying sedimentary layers from the erosional work performed on similar sediments on surrounding lands. Occupying low spots in the ir-

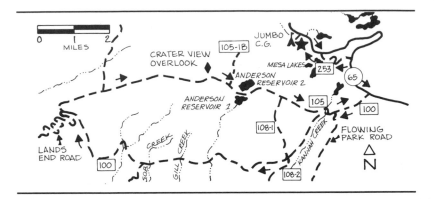

regular surface of frozen lava, more than 200 lakes are scattered about the plateau's 50 square miles.

In summer the wildflowers on the mesa are unbeatable: columbine, lupine, scarlet gilia, mule-ear and showy daisies, wild geranium, Indian paintbrush. In autumn, the turning aspens are equally colorful. The ride begins and ends at Jumbo Campground; alternately, you can start and finish at the road fork at mile 3.8, making it an easy-rated ride of 21.5 miles. The Grand Mesa's relatively subdued yet high-elevation terrain is a good place to begin acclimatizing to Colorado's breathtaking altitudes.

Jumbo Campground is 11 miles south of—and nearly a mile above!—the town of Mesa, on State Highway 65.

Spin out of the campground, turning right onto State Highway 65. Just past mile marker 36, at 0.6 mile, turn right onto Forest Road 253. Pass Mesa Lakes at 0.8 and start up steeply. At 1.7 curve hard left through a canopy of aspen. At 2.4 miles crest the rim, and turn right onto State Highway 65.

Ride along the rolling highway for 1.5 miles, then, at 3.8, turn right onto Forest Road 100/Lands End Road. Follow the wide and gently graded road, passing Flowing Park Road on the left at 5.0 and Forest Road 105 on the right at 5.2 (the latter is the road on which you'll close the loop). At 5.4 you reap terrific views downvalley to the left.

At 7.1 miles Forest Road 108-1 heads right and Forest Road 108-2 goes left; continue straight along the primary Forest Road 100. At 9.7 top out on the edge of the rim and at 10.7, after crossing Gill Creek, you can spot distant Uncompahgre Plateau through the gunsight notch in the hills. Cross S.O.B. Creek at 11.4 miles and at 13.4 pass by a road going left to Coal Creek Overlook. At 13.9 the peninsula of land dropping down from Lands End comes into view; note zigzag-ging Lands End Road switchbacking down its spine.

At 15.1 miles Lands End Road goes left; bear right, staying to the right of the stone visitors center. (Note: Lands End Road offers one of the all-time great downhills, losing 5,000 feet in 12 miles, along no fewer than 18 switchbacks.) At 15.5 the road becomes narrower. At 16.8, as the main road curves left, continue straight onto a much more primitive road that is rutted and rocky in spots.

Continue straight as a rugged road forks left at 17.2 miles; top out at 18.0, where primitive paths head both left and right. At 20.0 Crater View overlook is on the left; from here you can look down on the top of the Powderhorn ski area. At 20.8 coast into a meadow, with the back side of a dam on the left. Here Forest Road 105-1B goes left. At 21.3 miles Anderson Reservoir 2 is on the left and 1 is on the right.

At 22.3 miles continue straight as Forest Road 108-1 goes right. At 23.5 coast down and curve right across Kannah Creek. Continue bearing right as another road forks left; at 23.8 turn left, returning to Forest Road 100. At 25.3 turn left onto State Highway 65, retracing your tread tracks to Jumbo Campground, at 29.1 miles.

Crested Butte

In the 1950s Crested Butte, like a hundred other Colorado min-ing camps, was a has-been town. Only the rising popularity of its downhill ski area in the '70s helped it reattain the population level it had experienced during the heyday 1880s.

In the 1970s, Crested Butte was a focal point for the rebirth of the venerable telemark skiing turn. At the same time, to as large a degree as anywhere, mountain biking was born in this secluded, down-to-earth mountain village. The legend is told far and wide.

One summer day in 1976, several macho motorcyclists from As-pen swaggered into Crested Butte's Grubstake Bar, having just ridden their machines the 40 rough-and-tumble miles separating their home-town and Crested Butte. Their crowning achievement was the cresting of 12,705-foot Pearl Pass.

Not to be outdone by a bunch of motorheads from glitter city, a few weeks later a small contingent of Crested Butte adventurers/ski bums/wildfire-fighters pedaled their one-speed, fat-tire town bikes—or klunkers—over the pass and into Aspen, turning the motorcyclists' ad-venture into a mean feat.

Though they didn't know it at the time, the hardy crew had started a tradition, become cult heroes, and set the stage for Crested

Butte's emergence as the mountain-bike epicenter of the Rockies. Now, scores of mountain bikers take part in the annual Pearl Pass Tour each September, and hundreds join in the fun every July at Crested Butte's Fat Tire Bike Week. While in town, enthusiasts can pay homage to the first Pearl Pass Tour and other mountain-biking milestones by visiting the National Mountain Bike Hall of Fame and Museum. Hungry for summer dollars, the ski town has joyfully embraced mountain biking—you'll feel right at home and very welcome rolling into Crested Butte on fat tires.

"The Butte" is also "the Wildflower Capital of Colorado"—and this is not simply a hollow slogan dreamed up by the visitors bureau. The governor of the state actually proclaimed it so. The following rides, tracing gravel roads and single-track trails, penetrate splendid mountain scenery and traverse slopes covered in rainbows of wildflowers during July and August. They represent a cross-section of the dozens of nearby mountain-bike routes waiting to meet with your tires. It's truly a magical experience to mountain bike here.

The supplemental map needed for Crested Butte is the Gunnison National Forest visitors map, available through the Forest Supervisor's Office, 2250 Highway 50, Delta, CO 81416, (303) 874-7691, and at district offices in Paonia, Gunnison, and Montrose.

17. Oh-Be-Joyful

Riding surface:	Pavement, smooth gravel, rocky jeep trail
Elevation range:	8,909 to 10,000 feet
Distance:	20.8 miles
Relative difficulty:	Moderate
Time to allow:	3 to 5 hours
Best time of year:	July through September
Supplemental map:	Gunnison National Forest visitors map

The ride up the Oh-Be-Joyful Creek drainage is a fine introduction to the area, and a beautiful place to give thanks for having arrived at the nirvana of Rocky Mountain fat-tire biking. The narrative begins in downtown Crested Butte; you can reduce the ride's distance by 10.6 miles (for a total of 10.2 miles ridden) by beginning at the turnoff to Oh-Be-Joyful Road, at 5.3 miles.

Start in downtown Crested Butte at the corner of Elk Avenue and Gothic Road/State Highway 135.

Head north on Gothic Road. At 0.8 mile turn left onto Forest Road 734/Slate River Road, a wide and smooth gravel road. At 3.2

The smile says it all.

continue straight across the cattle guard (left goes onto private property). At 4.2, now well above river level, on the left in a grove of trees you can spot some pleasant, primitive camping spots. Forking left at 4.3 is Forest Road 585, a steep and rugged jeep road that loops over Gunsight Pass.

At 5.3 miles, turn left downhill onto Forest Road 754/Oh-Be-

Joyful Road. At the bottom, at 5.7, curve right away from the undeveloped campsites and ford bone-chilling Slate River. Once across
the water, bear left, following for 0.1 mile the indistinct path worn in
the river cobbles, and then climb steeply up the apparent road.

Ahead, at 6.6, where you break out onto a bench of rocks, are
good views of two waterfalls along Oh-Be-Joyful Creek. At 6.9
go straight rather than following the left fork. Continue up and
down, skirting rocky outcrops and spinning through meadows possibly
muddy in spots. Note on the surrounding, steep slopes that huge
swaths have been cleared by avalanches. At 10.2 pass an old cabin on
the left; continue gently uphill to the turnaround point at a stream
crossing, at 10.4 miles.

Circle back, and be joyful that it's downhill nearly all the way to
town!

18. Colorado Gothic

Riding surface:	Pavement, gravel, dirt road
Elevation range:	9,120 to 11,250 feet
Distance:	24.8 miles
Relative difficulty:	Moderate
Time to allow:	4 to 6 hours
Best time of year:	July through September
Supplemental map:	Gunnison National Forest visitors map

Don't leave Colorado without accomplishing this gem, which
shows off some of the state's finest scenery. You pass through the old
silver-mining town of Gothic, wildest of the wild 1880s Gunnison
County camps. The town, honored by a visit from President Grant in
1880, served as a staging area for servicing the smaller camps—such as
Aspen—lying over the surrounding mountain passes. Completely abandoned by 1930, for the last half century Gothic has been home of the
Rocky Mountain Biological Laboratory, established for the purpose of
studying high-elevation flora and fauna. The ride is best done on a
weekday.

Begin in Mount Crested Butte, at the junction of Gothic and
Treasury roads.

Pedal north, uphill, on paved Gothic Road. At 0.9 mile the road
surface turns to gravel. At 1.5 pass through a gate, where the road is
signed "County 317," and onto Gunnison National Forest lands.
(Demonstrating the area's commitment to mountain biking, this in-
the-middle-of-nowhere road also is signed as a bike route!) At 2.1 be-

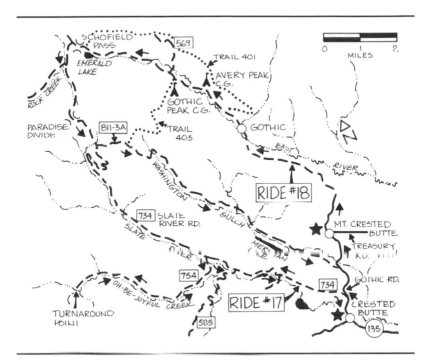

gin descending through a canopy of aspen. At 4.8 zip across the East River and into Gothic.

After climbing steeply out of Gothic, the road levels off at 5.5 miles. At 5.7 pass Trail 401, one of the area's most popular single-track riding trails, on the left. Avery Peak Campground is on the right at 6.6 and Gothic Peak Campground on the left at 7.1. Passing Forest Road 569/Rustlers Road going right at 7.7, begin a steep upgrade. At 8.2 miles cross the creek and begin the steep approach to Schofield Pass.

Go past the left-hand turn accessing sparkling Emerald Lake at 10.0, continuing steeply uphill for 0.75 mile to Schofield Pass, elevation 10,707 feet. Coast down and bear left at the fork toward Rock Creek. (Note: if you continue straight, you will descend one of the most notorious stretches of four-wheel-drive road in the Centennial State, and then pass through the settlements of Crystal and Marble. Slabs for national treasures such as the Lincoln Memorial and the Tomb of the Unknown Soldier were cut from nearby quarries.)

The road turns more primitive as it winds down into the creek bottom. At 11.5 miles bear left and climb steeply to 12.2. Pass through a couple of snowmelt streams, then start up the long, winding, switchbacking road. At 13.3, after a lot of work, you've finally reached

The view from Paradise (Divide, that is)

Paradise—Paradise Divide, that is—elevation 11,250 feet. Reward yourself by enjoying lunch while taking in the incredible view.

Continue along the road, heading down, down, down. At 14.5 turn left onto Washington Gulch Road/Forest Road 811-3A. (Note: you also can continue straight and return to town via the Slate River Road.) Spin along a stretch of alternating up and down, splashing through a couple of stream crossings en route. At 15.7 top out (Trail 403 goes left here, coming out north of Gothic). Bear left on the main road.

At 15.8 miles switchback right, away from the old buildings; pass by some more old cabins and mining remains at 16.1. The wildflowers along this stretch of open hillside can be fabulous. Hit two more stream crossings as you coast out on this smooth road. At 21.2 ride over a cattle guard, then pass through a gate at 21.5 and head downhill, with several houses off to the left. Roll by Meridian Lake and across a couple of cattle guards, then turn left onto Gothic Road at 23.7. Huff up the final grunt into Mount Crested Butte, returning to your beginning point at 24.8 miles.

19. Teocalli Ridge Run

Riding surface: Pavement, smooth gravel, rough jeep trail, single-track trail
Elevation range: 8,909 to 11,286 feet
Distance: 25.8 miles
Relative difficulty: Hard
Time to allow: 5 to 8 hours
Best time of year: July through September
Supplemental map: Gunnison National Forest visitors map

This is an extreme ride—a lung scorcher and a leg burner—with rewards to match. Included are plenty of tough climbs for the anaerobic animal and zippy downhills for the gravity hog, and enough cold stream crossings to make even the most amphibious of fat-tire freaks squeal like a seal.

The adventure begins in downtown Crested Butte, at the corner of Elk Avenue and State Highway 135/Gothic Road.

Pedal southeast on State Highway 135. At 2.2 miles turn left toward the airport onto Forest Road 738/Brush Creek Road. At 2.7 the surface turns to gravel as it proceeds gently uphill alongside the golf course. At 4.0 crest a high point and coast down to the bridge spanning the East River at 4.9 miles. At 5.2, as you pass corrals on the left, check out the spring with good drinking water on the right.

At 6.0 spin by a progression of ponds and at 6.8 pedal onto private property, the public-access road becoming steep and bumpy. At 7.3 pass through a gate onto the Ambush Ranch and at 7.8 miles bear left uphill onto Forest Road 738-2A toward West Brush Creek (right follows the main fork of Brush Creek, cresting Pearl Pass in 11 miles). Don't let the incredible scenery spread out in front cause you to forget to look at the scenery behind, for it's just as splendid.

At 8.4 pass through a gate; at the Y at 8.6, in an open meadow, follow the right fork toward West Brush Creek Trail (left goes to Deer Creek). At 8.9 pass through a gate and at 9.8 go through the creek, then follow the groove in the river cobbles back to the road, now running along the right side of the creek. At 11.2 coast across a small stream and begin steeply uphill, crossing numerous small drainages en route. At 11.5 the grade becomes walking steep.

At 12.0 miles, at a cairn and a wooden post, turn hard right onto a single-track trail. Most folks will need to walk the majority of the next mile plus. Accept it, take it easy, and enjoy the views; look closely for showy displays of the beautiful columbine, Colorado's state flower.

At 13.3 turn right onto single-track at the signs directing you toward Teocalli Ridge/Brush Creek, and continue uphill. At 14.0 miles break out onto an exposed ridge, with good views of Castle Mountain behind. The gunsight notch to the right of the mountain is legendary Pearl Pass. At 14.1 start the big downhill, winding first through coniferous forest, then through shimmering aspen groves. In spots the trail is washed out and precipitous; there's a slim chance of meeting a hiker coming up the hill, so proceed with caution.

At 15.3 miles bear straight/right toward Teocalli Ridge (left goes uphill toward Brush Creek) and continue down. At 16.3 break out of the aspens into a clearing and bear left at 16.8 at the watering hole. In 0.1 mile bear right downhill onto a smooth, primitive road. At 17.1 bear right on the main road as Trail 409 goes left to Farris Creek/ Cement Creek. At 17.4 come to a stream and bear right alongside it. In another 0.1 mile, at what appears to be a dead end, commit yourself to getting soaked and ride/walk through a long stretch of stream, then

Almost to the top!

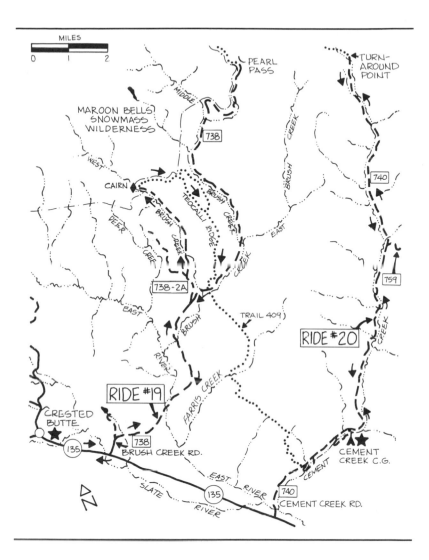

again pop up onto the road. After accomplishing another, shorter creek fording, bear left at the sign onto West Brush Creek Road.

Climb to 17.9 miles and start down, heading straight onto the road merging in from the left. At 18.1 close the loop, coming off Forest Road 738 and back onto Forest Road 738-2A. Head back from where you came, returning to the main junction in Crested Butte at 25.8 miles.

20. Cement Creek

Riding surface: Smooth gravel to rough dirt
Elevation range: 8,960 to 10,200 feet
Distance: 15.6 miles
Relative difficulty: Easy
Time to allow: 2 to 4 hours
Best time of year: July through September
Supplemental map: Gunnison National Forest visitors map

Much of the riding in the Crested Butte area is prohibitively tough for all but top-conditioned riders. This is my nomination for the Butte's break-in-the-buns/family/after-supper ride: it offers easy spinning, beautiful scenery, and a campground. Don't neglect it even if you're not a family or if your buns are already well worn—it's a delightful outing, regardless. Weekdays are the best.

From Crested Butte, go 7 miles southeast on State Highway 135, then 4 miles east on Cement Creek Road/Forest Road 740, to Cement Creek Campground. (Note: by beginning at the junction of State Highway 135 and Cement Creek Road, you'll add on 8 miles roundtrip. The additional 4-mile section of Cement Creek Road offers pleasant riding, but often carries more motorized traffic than does the stretch of road above the campground.)

From the campground, pedal northeast on Cement Creek Road/Forest Road 740, passing through a pinch in the terrain where the canyon narrows and the creek falls fast, frothing through its conglomerate-boulder-strewn bed. In just over 1 mile, on the right, spin by a picturesque old cattle ranch, once also a commercial hot-springs resort. Continue upstream, with steep hills rising on the left and Cement Creek's floodplain meadows on the right; a prettier spot would be hard to come by. At 2.6 miles the public-access road passes onto a stretch of private land.

At 3.9 pass through a gate; the road becomes much rougher as it enters a tight redrock canyon. Parallel the tumbling creek and cross it at 4.5; climb and switchback right, then left, as the canyon opens up. At the junction, bear left on Cement Creek Road/Forest Road 740 where Forest Road 759 goes right.

Cross through a stream at 5.5, and another at 6.2 miles. Crest a high point at 7.1, then coast down through a third stream crossing at 7.4. Beyond this point conditions begin to "climb" well above the easy-rated range, but push on at least to 7.8, where the impressive Collegiate Peaks pop into view.

The road continues for 3 or 4 miles, becoming progressively more steep and rugged. Proceed if the spirit and legs are willing, for the scenery is outstanding. Otherwise, turn around and coast back to the campground, rediscovered at 15.6 miles.

Durango–Purgatory

Purgatory. Webster's defines it as "an intermediate state" or "a place of temporary punishment." But there's nothing unsettled or punishing about this Purgatory. As do the downhill skiers who visit the slopes of Purgatory ski area each winter, you'll be calling the area "Heaven" after a few days of mountain biking here.

That plenty of Hollywood producers have found the Durango-Purgatory area to their liking speaks for its rugged, classic Western landscape. Movies filmed in the vicinity include *Across the Wide Missouri* and *Butch Cassidy and the Sundance Kid*.

The Purgatory ski area rents mountain bikes and offers chair-lift rides—to both bikes and riders—to the top of the mountain, providing the thrill of descent without the sweat of ascent. The ski area has become a popular venue for mountain-bike racing, and in September of 1990 hosted the first officially sanctioned mountain bike world championships.

The supplemental map needed for the area surrounding Purgatory is the San Juan National Forest visitors map, available through the Forest Supervisor's Office, 701 Camino del Rio, Durango, CO 81301, (303) 247-4874, and at district offices in Mancos, Bayfield, Dolores, and Pagosa Springs.

21. Lime Creek Cliffhanger

Riding surface: Rough gravel, pavement
Elevation range: 8,796 to 10,630 feet
Distance: 19.3 miles
Relative difficulty: Moderate
Time to allow: 3 to 4 hours
Best time of year: June through September
Supplemental map: San Juan National Forest visitors map

Lime Creek Road, originally a stretch of the main highway connecting Durango and Silverton, was abandoned in 1959 for the route over Coal Bank Pass. Now badly deteriorated, motorists find it miserable but mountain bikers call it magnificent. If you prefer not to close

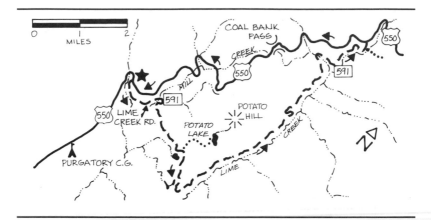

the loop by riding on sometimes-bustling U.S. Highway 550 (which has a 1- to 3-foot paved shoulder), either do a pre-ride vehicle shuttle or backtrack along 11.1-mile-long Lime Creek Road. Otherwise, follow the narrative all the way through for a complete loop.

The adventure begins 2.2 miles north of Purgatory Campground. Just beyond the guard rail on a big curve, pull into the parking area on the east side of the road, at the Potato Lake Trail sign.

Commence riding on Lime Creek Road, heading uphill among the aspen. At 0.9 mile a primitive track merges from the left; at 2.3 miles pass along a big rock face as the road itself becomes quite rocky. At 2.9 burst into a clearing beside a big, active beaver pond; continue up the bumpy-surfaced road, topping out at 3.7 miles.

At 4.0 begin along a platform chiseled into the face of a cliff, with old rock-work guard rails between you and the long fall down into the Lime Creek bottoms. At 4.4 start plunging steeply, arriving at creek level at 5.6 miles. Paralleling the creek upstream, roll past some inviting, undeveloped campsites. At 6.6 commence climbing more steeply, away from the creek.

At 7.5 switchback left, then right, through a big avalanche chute; at 8.3 curve right through the drainage, beginning a rocky uphill (note the waterfalls across the valley). Leveling off in a forest of aspen and spruce, at 9.0 spot the new highway ahead and above. At 9.3 pass over a bridge, viewing a rocky chasm to the left; at 9.9 top out and start down. At 11.1 miles, curve left at the Y, then turn left onto U.S. Highway 550, beginning a long uphill stretch.

Pass by a couple of tumbling waterfalls en route to Coal Bank Pass, elevation 10,630 feet, crested at 14.1 miles. Here you begin a long and fun downhill. Ahead on the right is Engineer Mountain, elevation

Moonrise over Twilight Peak

12,968 feet. A *nunatak*—a peak that protruded above the Pleistocene icecap, thereby escaping glaciation—Engineer's jagged nature contrasts sharply with the surrounding smooth and rounded high country. Return to the ride's beginning point at 19.3 miles.

22. Graysill Ghostbuster

Riding surface:	Smooth gravel, rocky jeep trail
Elevation range:	8,850 to 11,000 feet
Distance:	27.9 miles
Relative difficulty:	Moderate
Time to allow:	4 to 6 hours
Best time of year:	July through September
Supplemental map:	San Juan National Forest visitors map

The Graysill mining camp was active between 1945 and 1963, when vanadium (used to harden steel) and uranium ores were sought. Now a backcountry ghost town, it's visited only by a few hardy moun-

Talus slope, Graysill Mountain

tain bikers and intrepid motorists. To endure the jolting approach, the motorist must be nearly as determined as the mountain biker.

If you want to camp along the loop, Sig Creek Campground (mile 24.7) makes a good starting/ending point.

The ride demands some rather tricky navigating where two roads are linked together by a hard-to-find trail. If you are not up for an orienteering session, or if you'd simply prefer an easier outing, pedal down Forest Road 579 and Forest Road 580 for a terrific out-and-back. Evening mountain light plays magic on the timber stands and rocky outcrops and talus slopes.

From Purgatory Campground, cross the highway and head toward the ski area; follow Forest Road 578 steeply uphill for 4 miles, to its junction with Forest Road 579.

From the junction of Forest Road 578 and Forest Road 579, go right on Forest Road 579. Pedal gradually uphill under a canopy of aspen, along the smooth gravel road. Continue straight/left at 0.2 mile as another road forks steeply uphill to the right. At 1.1 bear straight onto Forest Road 580, a narrower road with a different-colored surface, as Forest Road 579 curves abruptly to the right.

At 2.1 curve left; note, as you switch aspect, the forest cover changing from predominantly aspen to one including more spruce. Topping out, there's a good view on the left of the back side of Purgatory ski area. It's up and down during the next few miles. At 5.2, after rounding a left-hand curve, meet Grayrock Peak, elevation 12,504 feet, on the right. At 6.3 curve left through a talus slope at the base of Grayrock, and check out the long-distance views to the left.

The road continues winding up and down over ridges and through drainages. At 9.9 miles turn right uphill, passing through a closed gate. (Note: the road you're turning off becomes more primitive and continues for another 1.5 miles before dead-ending at a terrific streamside campsite.) Commence climbing steadily over the rough and grassy old road surface.

At 11.2 the path levels as it bisects a big talus slope on the flanks of Graysill Mountain. At 11.5 miles head straight up a steep 80 yard pitch, rather than bearing downhill to the left. At 12.4 the grade decreases as you begin rolling through a series of old clearcuts; keep an eye out for deadfall timber on the path. At 13.5 go straight (left) rather than right uphill.

At 14.0 miles, at the end of the clearcuts, the faint path peters out altogether. Walk downhill to the left, keeping on the right side of the little creek. (A wise move: leave your bike above and locate the trail first, then retrieve the trusty mount.) In approximately 120 yards, you'll spot a good, narrow trail heading sharply right into the woods.

At 14.1, where the trail exits the woods, take the upper right-hand choice at the road switchback. At 14.4 walk your bike through the talus-filled drainage, and arrive at the old Graysill Mine at 14.5. (Note: from the mine it's a 2-mile round trip to scenic Bolam Pass.) Start down steeply from the mine site on rough-surfaced Forest Road 578. In 1 mile, sweep along the red-surfaced road through a series of five pairs of switchback turns. At 16.6, after the final pair, the downhill grade diminishes.

At 19.2 ride through a stream and begin traversing wide-open floodplain. At 19.8 climb above the creek, passing at 20.2 several nice, undeveloped campsites. Continue straight at 20.4 where Forest Road 550 goes right toward Hotel Draw. (Note: in what would be an intriguing ride, four-wheel-drive Forest Road 550 crests the mountain ridge to the west, then follows Scotch Creek out to State Highway 145, just south of the town of Rico.)

At 21.2 cross through wide—and deep, if prior to mid-July—Hermosa Creek. Continue gradually down to 22.2, then start up. At 22.4 cross a cattle guard, following the road as it veers left away from the main fork of Hermosa Creek and heads upstream along the creek's east fork. At 22.8 is the access road going to the trailhead for the Hermosa Creek Trail (where ride 23 begins). Here, the road surface becomes suitable for all vehicles under all weather conditions.

Pass Sig Creek Campground on the left at 24.7. Rolling along the East Fork's wide floodplain, skirt the back side of Purgatory ski area at 25.8 miles. At 26.8, just beyond a cattle guard crossing, the climb steepens. The grade diminishes and the loop closes at 27.9 miles.

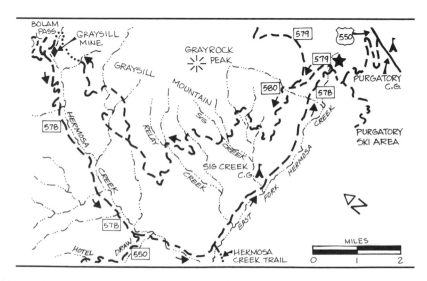

23. Hermosa Creek Trail

Riding surface: Single-track trail, gravel road, pavement
Elevation range: 6,640 to 8,840 feet
Distance: 23.1 miles
Relative difficulty: Moderate
Time to allow: 4 to 7 hours
Best time of year: July through September
Supplemental map: San Juan National Forest visitors map

Hermosa, a Spanish word meaning "beautiful" or "pretty," describes this outing well. The scenery is pretty, the creek is pretty, and the ride is "pretty" hard.

It's also pretty tiring. If you want to make it *really* tiring, plan to accomplish a complete loop by pedaling the 16 road miles, mostly uphill with good shoulder, from the village of Hermosa back to Purgatory Campground. Otherwise, shuttle a vehicle and leave it at ride's end.

Among the finest single-track rides in Colorado, the trail is also open to motorcycles. By riding midweek, you'll avoid encountering many.

These three items, all relating to water, you should consider carrying along: (1) a water filter, for if your bottles run dry, it will be a particularly thirsty experience watching the creek—the water from which shouldn't be drunk untreated—rushing alongside mile after mile; (2) some stream-crossing treads, if you'd rather not get those shiny new mountain-bike shoes drenched; and (3) your fishing pole.

Because of the often narrow and/or steep nature of the trail, carrying panniers stuffed with camping gear would make this ride really tough. There are some terrific streamside campsites along the first 6 miles of trail, before the more technical sections ensue. If you want to camp, consider simply pedaling in a few miles and backtracking out the next day.

From Purgatory Campground, cross the highway and drive 9 miles (4 up, 5 down) on Forest Road 578 to Hermosa Park. The trailhead parking area is on the left.

Ride onto the signed trail, at 0.1 mile passing through a gate, closing it behind you, and onto private land. Coast from woods into meadow at 0.6 and re-enter USFS land at 0.8. Ride through a second gate at 1.8 miles.

Pass a primitive campsite at 2.5; at 3.1 Corral Draw Trail goes right. Whiz by a stretch of picture-perfect fishing holes in the 4.0 vicinity; climb to 4.3 and coast down to the first stream crossing, at 4.8

Hermosa Creek Trail, among the finest single-track rides in Colorado

miles. (Here, Elbert Creek Trail continues along the east side of the creek as you follow along its west side.)

Pass through gate number three at 5.1. At 5.7, rather than heading straight up the short, steep pitch, bear left and again ride through the creek. From 6.5 to 8.4 miles negotiate a stretch containing some tricky sidehilling (don't look down). Switchback right through a drainage at 8.5 and begin climbing high above the creek level.

Start a long downhill at 9.8, passing through a gate at 10.2. Note that, as you lose elevation, gambel oak is becoming more abundant. Also feel the temperature rising, if it's a sunny summer day.

Hook right through a draw at 10.3; top out at 10.5 and roll along a pleasantly winding stretch of trail. Heading steeply down, bottom out at 11.1 miles where the South Fork Hermosa Trail goes right; begin up. Hook right through Little Elk Creek at 11.6. Continue repeating this mantra: up, through the drainage, and down; up, through the drainage, and down.

At 13.5 miles begin a long and twisting descent ending at 14.0, where the Clear Creek Trail goes right. At 14.1 cross the Dutch Creek bridge, a good spot to refill water bottles, and start up the longest and meanest hill of the route—a walker. At 15.0 curve right through the head of a draw in a beautiful aspen stand. Continue climbing to 15.1; from that point it's mostly down to a draw-crossing at 15.6 miles. Continue winding up and through draws along this south-facing hillside, which is covered with pine and oak trees.

At 17.7 miles ride steeply into a side drainage, watching for diagonally placed water bars just beyond—they're potential wipe-out enhancers. Swing right through a couple of little draws at 18.5, and at 18.7 follow the left/uphill fork, popping up onto Forest Road 576. Commence cruising down this high-grade gravel road; at 21.0 miles hit pavement. Cross a cattle guard at 21.7 and arrive at U.S. Highway 550 in Hermosa at 23.1 miles.

Pretty good ride, huh?

Pagosa Springs–South Fork

Pagosa Springs, made famous by the country song in which the good-buddy 18-wheeler loses his brakes descending Wolf Creek Pass and blasts through downtown, is becoming a primary tourist-servicing center. There are mountain-bike rentals and fat-tire group tours available through local shops; other convenient diversions include Rio Grande river-running expeditions, guided tours of nearby Chimney Rock Archaeological Area (an Anasazi Indian ruin), and a soak at Great Pagosa Hot Spring Park.

South Fork, just northeast across Wolf Creek Pass from Pagosa, sits at the confluence of the Rio Grande's south and main forks. Between here and Creede and Lake City, to the north, lies some of the most dramatic mountain scenery in the Lower 48; the High Lonesome Loop (ride 25) is just a teaser of what's out there, waiting. In the few

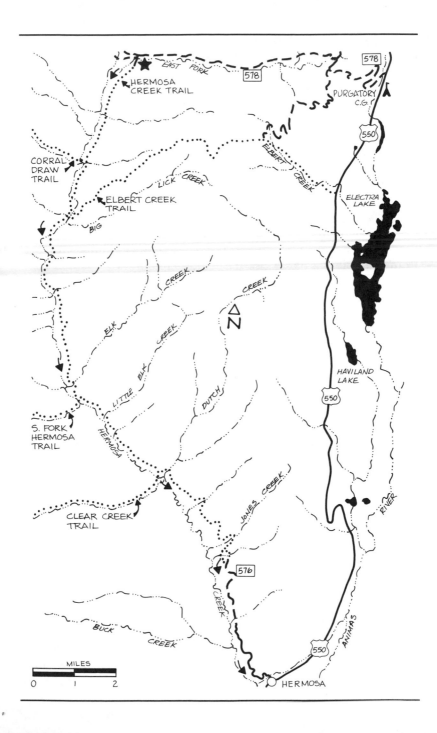

hundred square miles immediately surrounding South Fork are more potential loops than you can shake a pump at. Pore over the visitors map and you'll get the picture.

The supplemental map needed for the Pagosa Springs area is the San Juan National Forest visitors map, available through the Forest Supervisor's Office, 701 Camino del Rio, Durango, CO 81301, (303) 247-4874, and at district offices in Mancos, Bayfield, Dolores, and Pagosa Springs. For South Fork, pick up the Rio Grande National Forest visitors map, available through the Forest Supervisor's Office, 1803 West Highway 160, Monte Vista, CO 81144, (719) 852-5941, and at district offices in La Jara, Creede, and Saguache.

24. Willow Draw Loop

Riding surface:	Pavement, gravel, four-wheel-drive trail
Elevation range:	7,120 to 7,770 feet
Distance:	15.8 miles
Relative difficulty:	Easy
Time to allow:	2 to 4 hours
Best time of year:	May through October
Supplemental map:	San Juan National Forest visitors map

Willow Draw is a nifty little loop out of a neat little town. The initial stretch of the ride, along U.S. Highway 160, parallels the San Juan River. The river rises just a few miles above Pagosa Springs on the mountain divide, flows south into New Mexico, then bends northwest and runs through Navajo country and just north of the point where the Four Corners states meet.

On the primitive-road sections of the loop are several spots where you could go wrong; most of these are posted "No Motor Vehicles." The clay soils on this route make it impassable during or after a substantial rainfall.

Park near the junction of U.S. Highway 160 and U.S. Highway 84, at the east edge of Pagosa Springs.

Pedal northeast on the wide shoulder of U.S. Highway 160, skirting picturesque floodplain ranchlands along the San Juan River. At 1.3, on the right, is a commercial campground; at 1.8, for those desiring more in their accommodations, is a bed-and-breakfast guest ranch. Top out at 2.4 and head down; at 3.5 turn right onto Fawn Gulch Road/County 113/Forest Road 666. Head uphill on this wide gravel road.

Pass over a cattle guard at 3.9 and continue up. At 4.5 miles cross

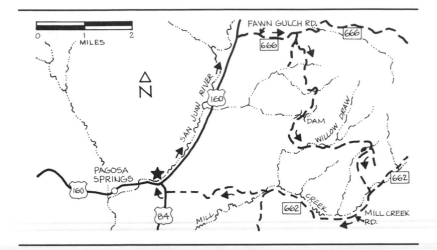

a second cattle guard; approximately 100 yards beyond, turn right off the main road, dropping onto a primitive track. Heading up, spin by some pleasant, undeveloped campsites among the ponderosa pines. At 4.8 miles bear left at the fork. Cross a draw at 5.1 and continue down. At 5.8 ride up a short hill, topping out at 6.3 with long-range views of distant mesas to the south.

After a rolling stretch that includes some steeper uphills, top out on the side of a small ridge at 6.6; at 6.8 continue on the uphill fork. After winding down a hill, at 7.4 pedal over the top of a dam spanning the drainage, and bear right. At 7.6 miles curve hard left uphill, topping out in 50 yards. At 7.7 cross Willow Draw, then head upstream along its right side.

At 8.2 bear right away from the draw and pass through a gate on a short, steep uphill. Go through a second gate in 50 yards; some terrific camping spots sit along this ponderosa pine-covered ridgetop. Still heading upstream, at 8.8 veer right along the southernmost creek branch; at 9.5 miles top out, curve right, and head down. At 9.6, where a primitive track forks to the left uphill, continue straight with a pond on your right.

After heading down a narrow little draw, veer left and climb a short hill at 10.2. With the looming San Juan peaks rising into the sky behind you, head down, splashing through Mill Creek at 10.6. At 10.7 turn right onto Mill Creek Road/Forest Road 662. Wind gently downstream through the pastoral valley on high-grade road. At 15.6 turn right onto U.S. Highway 84, returning to the junction in downtown Pagosa Springs at 15.8 miles.

25. High Lonesome Loop

Riding surface: Smooth gravel, rough jeep trail
Elevation range: 8,825 to 11,480 feet
Distance: 23.7 miles
Relative difficulty: Hard
Time to allow: 4 to 7 hours
Best time of year: July through September
Supplemental map: Rio Grande National Forest visitors map

On this ride you may spot a group of elk bedded down in an alpine basin, or a herd of high-mountain bovines grazing in a lush meadow. But you likely won't run into many two-legged beasts. The ride begins and ends at Cross Creek Campground, near the shores of Beaver Creek Reservoir. If the basic 23.7-mile loop isn't enough—it will be for all but the hyper-ambitious—tack on the 4.6-mile round trip to Poage Lake.

From the town of South Fork, go 1 mile south on U.S. Highway 160 and turn left onto Beaver Creek Road/Forest Road 20. Cross Creek Campground is approximately 6.5 miles up this road; en route, you also pass by Beaver Creek and Upper Beaver Creek campgrounds.

Leave Cross Creek Campground and turn left onto Forest Road 20, heading up a steep hill. Switchback left at 0.6 and, at 1.2 miles, turn left onto Forest Road 359 toward Cross Creek, heading uphill on this initially high-grade road.

At 1.8 curve left as a primitive road goes right up-draw; switchback right at 2.4, then left at 3.3. Note the forest cover changing as the altitude rises. At 6.3 miles follow the left fork as another path veers uphill to the right. At 6.9 go over Cross Creek, then switchback left and right as the grade steepens.

At 7.6 miles continue straight on Forest Road 359 where Forest Road 350 goes up steeply to the left. (Note: Forest Road 350 itself offers an intriguing ride, coming out just east of South Fork.) Your once-smooth road, rapidly deteriorating into a rough-and-tumble jeep trail, leads to 8.5, where big, snow-clad peaks pop into view across the valley.

At 9.3 the route becomes very rutted; at 9.6, where ruts head in several directions, follow the wooden guideposts stuck in the ground. Crest the ride's high point beside a pond at 9.7, then pass through a gate and begin the steep and twisting downhill. Stop first, however, and take in the view, perhaps the most splendid this side of Switzerland. Yodel to your heart's content; no one will hear!

At the bottom of the rocky downhill, follow the track as it winds

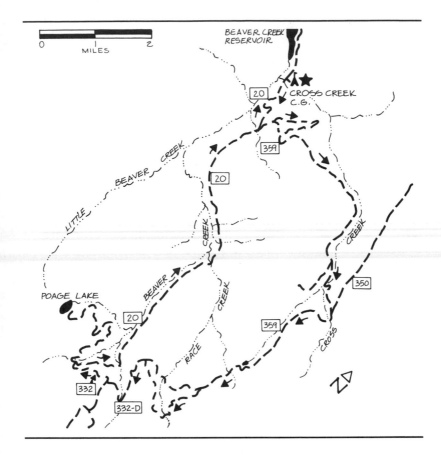

through lush meadow. At 11.0 miles take the left fork, coasting down and through the little creek; immediately bear right onto the indistinct path heading through the meadow toward a stand of timber. (On this path you climb above, at an angle of about 90 degrees to, the creek and the road paralleling it downstream.) At 11.1 the path enters the timber, becoming a bit more obvious. At the T at 11.2 miles turn left uphill onto an old logging road. At 11.5, after a steep little grind, top out and merge right/straight onto a more distinct road, then begin contouring around an old clearcut.

Start down at 11.8 miles, the road quality improving at 12.3. (At 13.6, to the right, is where you would have ended up if you'd followed

"Slow elk"

the right fork back at 11.0.) Curve hard right to cross the creek at 14.4, and at 14.9 top out and turn right onto Forest Road 332. Head down on the gray-colored, gravel-surfaced road.

At 15.1 curve right through a draw, glimpsing the valley below where you're headed. At 15.8 turn right onto Forest Road 20. (Note: to go to Poage Lake, turn left. It's 2.3 miles on high-grade road to the parking lot, from which the lake is a short hike away.) Begin a long, smooth, *fun* downhill through the pretty valley, bottoming out at 22.2 miles. At 22.5 pass the turn to Cross Creek, closing the loop, and at 23.7 miles return to Cross Creek Campground.

Other Rides in Colorado

After experiencing some of the preceding rides, no doubt you'll agree there's not a better place to mountain bike than southwest Colorado. Study the various forest visitors maps, and you'll see that the options truly are almost endless. To help narrow down the possibilities, here are a few recommendations for other rides—or at least good places to start looking.

Colorado Trail. The 469-mile Colorado Trail spans the mountain fastness separating Denver and Durango. Though the trail lies mostly on federal lands, its concept and construction were largely the work of volunteers, and its funding derived from donations. The visionary trail planners anticipated the boom in mountain biking and—although it necessitated extra work—early on chose to map a route for mountain bikers as well as for the more traditional hikers, equestrians, and skiers.

The primary hiking trail passes through several wilderness areas; in each case a map delineates a mountain-bike detour, utilizing jeep paths and county roads to skirt the off-limits wilderness. Outside of wilderness areas, the trail for mountain bikers is the same as for others.

Simply because it's designated for mountain biking doesn't mean that just anyone should head out aiming to ride the length of the trail. Many sections encompass ultra-technical riding conditions, at elevations commonly exceeding 12,000 feet. The trail guidebook warns, "In addition [to the off-limits wilderness areas], there are other areas where cyclists may end up pushing their bikes more than riding them, especially if they are loaded down with gear." And that's a fact.

The maps and guidebook for the Colorado Trail are available through the Colorado Trail Foundation, P.O. Box 260876, Lakewood, CO 80226.

Kokopelli's Trail. Another long-distance route, Kokopelli's Trail winds 128 miles from just west of Grand Junction to Moab, Utah. The trail—named after the Hopi Indians' humped-back, flute-playing god of fertility—bisects desert lands and crests the high La Sal Mountains. The mountain-bike-specific trail was developed by a cooperative arrangement among the Bureau of Land Management, the U.S. Forest Service, and the Colorado Plateau Mountain-Bike Trail Association (also known as COPMOBA—it seems that it's a requirement for all mountain-bike clubs to be known by their acronyms). Most of the trail follows existing county and four-wheel-drive roads, with 10 miles of new single-track constructed to tie together the complete route.

The nonprofit COPMOBA plans to tackle additional projects just as ambitious, including a trail winding south from Grand Junction across the Uncompahgre Plateau and ending at Montrose. Information on Kokopelli's Trail and planned future developments is available through COPMOBA, P.O. Box 4602, Grand Junction, CO 81502, (303) 241-9561.

San Juan Range. Some outstanding mountain-biking opportunities lie in the rugged, expansive San Juan Range between South Fork and Lake City. In the San Juan National Forest, check out some of the primitive roads around Wagon Wheel Gap, such as Forest Road 600, which leads to the Wheeler Geologic Area, a place of eerily eroded, pink-and-white volcanic-tuff cones and spires; the Forest Road 503-Forest Road 504 loop immediately north of Creede; the series of forest roads looping south from Marshall Park Campground, 7 miles southwest of Creede; and South Clear Creek Road/Forest Road 515, beginning approximately 22 miles west of Creede on State Highway 149.

A mountain-biking paradise, the San Juan Triangle lies west of Lake City on lands administered by the Bureau of Land Management. The main triangle of 45 miles follows a route originally built in the late nineteenth century for miners' wagons. Also popular with four-wheel-drive enthusiasts, the loop crests 12,620-foot Cinnamon Pass and 12,800-foot Engineer Pass (neither of which are *quite* as bad as they sound, for the "low" point on the loop—Lake City—is at 8,600 feet).

The triangle has been added to the BLM's Scenic Backcountry Byways program. The ensuing publicity may result—on occasional summer days—in motorized-traffic counts unacceptable to peace-and-quiet-loving mountain bikers. But don't let that prevent you from at least driving parts of the loop and sampling some of the many spur routes branching off the main triangle. (Four-wheel drive is necessary in order to drive the complete loop.) Suggestions: the Carson Trail, following a jeep road to one of the best-preserved ghost towns in the San Juans—Carson, that is, which had its heyday in the 1890s; Cottonwood Creek Road, penetrating a steep-walled canyon reminiscent of a little Yosemite Valley; American Basin, with its incredible display of wildflowers in July and August; and the short side-trip to Animas Forks ghost town, which once boasted the highest post office in America at 11,200 feet and, in 1884, endured a 23-day blizzard that smothered the town in 25 feet of snow.

For a terrific map and informational handout on the San Juan Triangle, contact the Gunnison Resource Area BLM, 216 North Colorado, Gunnison, CO 81230, (303) 641-0471. Request the *Alpine Explorer* brochure.

(Note: this is Alferd Packer country. During the murderous winter of 1874, snowbound with fellow prospectors on a high-mountain ridge near Lake City, Packer killed his companions and ate their flesh to stay alive. He was found guilty of murder in 1883; however, due to a technicality, the conviction was overturned three years later and his crime was reduced to five counts of manslaughter. Watch behind the trees, for Packer's ghost may remain. . . .)

Ouray–Telluride area. On Uncompahgre National Forest lands, the Ouray–Telluride area offers high-elevation pedaling amidst dramatic landscape. Although known as the "Switzerland of America," the region shouldn't be held up for comparison to other places in the world—the other locales should be compared to here. It's a corner of America that must be seen to be believed.

From Ouray, it's possible—for the fit—to ride to Telluride over extremely rugged Imogene Pass. And even the fittest of cyclists will do some heavy breathing on this ride, for Imogene crests at higher than 13,000 feet.

Beginning on the south side of Red Mountain Pass, south of Ouray along U.S. Highway 550, is a good one- or two-day loop. Pedaling west over Black Bear Pass, you follow a jeep road that falls drastically down a set of switchbacks—something of a local legend and landmark—at the head of the Telluride valley. The narrow road is one-way going west for jeeps; a chance meeting with a westbound jeep would mean, for the eastbound driver, having to back down the hairpins all the way to the valley below. (And how would one do this? *Very* carefully.)

An overnight at one of the historic lodgings in Telluride will rest you for the return trip down State Highway 145, east over the Ophir

Pass jeep road, and north along U.S. Highway 550 back to the beginning point.

From Engineer Pass on the San Juan Triangle (see above) it's also possible to drop—almost literally, as you lose 5,000 feet in 10 miles—into Ouray. Likewise, from near Cinnamon Pass, you can coast south into Silverton, paralleling the Animas River downstream.

Similar to the hut-to-hut systems designed for cross-country ski travel, a chain of shelters for mountain bikers is being developed between Telluride and Moab, Utah. The huts, spaced apart by about five hours' average riding time, contain food, cooking equipment, and bedding, thus allowing for very light mountain-bike travel. For information on the hut system, call (303) 728-6935.

Alpine Plateau. Also on the Uncompahgre National Forest and on adjacent BLM lands, check out the Alpine Plateau road system. Start on U.S. Highway 150 near Curecanti National Recreation Area, along the Gunnison River, approximately 10 miles west of Sapinero. Beginning at 8,500 feet in elevation, BLM Road 3004 climbs along Little Blue Creek's east fork. Becoming Forest Road 867 at the national forest boundary, the road tops out at 11,508 feet. It forks left at the junction with Forest Road 868 and, reclaiming its BLM Road 3004 designation, plunges downhill to meet State Highway 149 at a point 11 miles north of Lake City.

Roughly 10 miles north of this point, BLM Road 3009 makes an interesting yo-yo ride of about 15 miles round-trip. It pierces the canyon of the Gunnison River's Lake Fork as the stream makes its final approach to the confluence with the main fork.

Finally, 5 miles east of BLM Road 3009, BLM Road 3033 offers a fascinating ride through a mid-elevation landscape of scrub and badlands.

Pagosa Springs. In addition to ride 25 in this area, consider checking out Turkey Springs Road/Forest Road 629, as it leads from Piedra Road, at a point 9 miles northwest of town, south to U.S. Highway 160.

Another nominee, with rewarding views at the turnaround, begins 6 miles south of town on U.S. Highway 84. From this point, Forest Road 652 climbs to the west, to Eightmile Mesa Lookout Tower.

East Fork Road/Forest Road 667 heads eastward from a point 10 miles north of town on U.S. Highway 160. Presenting relatively easy cruising for the first 10 miles, it deteriorates into a four-wheel-drive road, climbing for several miles to reach Elwood Pass. At the pass you'll want to turn around and backtrack, or else commit to an expedition and continue down into the San Juan National Forest, heading in one of several directions: to the north, coming out at Park Creek Campground south of South Fork; to the northeast, rolling out at Del Norte; to the east, following the Alamosa River to a point just south of Monte Vista; or to the southeast, exiting the wilds at Elk Creek Campground along State Highway 17 between Chama, New Mexico, and Antonito, Colorado.

Finally, the ranger station in Pagosa Springs distributes a handout indicating which trails on the forest are open to motorcycles. Several of these offer good single-track riding.

Great Sand Dunes National Monument. Northeast of Alamosa, try the Medano Pass Road, a four-wheel-drive route. Along the lower portions of the route sand may inhibit forward motion, but as it gains elevation and climbs into the Sangre de Cristo Range the road offers first-class mountain biking.

Also recommended by National Park Service personnel are the Mosca Pass road/trail, climbing east from the monument into the Sangre de Cristos, and the Blanca Peak road/trail to the south. The latter, crossing mostly BLM and USFS lands, provides access to the trailheads for climbs to a couple of the Sangre de Cristos' "fourteeners" (peaks rising higher than 14,000 feet above sea level). The Rio Grande National Forest visitors map depicts Great Sand Dunes National Monument and surrounding lands.

Dolores area. At this writing, the Durango Resource Area of the BLM was developing mountain-biking opportunities in the Dolores area, very close to where the Four Corners states share a common point. For current information, call the Durango office at (303) 247-4082.

3
NEW MEXICO

In the other Four Corners states, landscape dominates the visitor's attention. In New Mexico it's the people and their cultures, and how they interact with their shining mountains and endless deserts, that prevail.

Crossing the border into northwest New Mexico is like coming into a new country. At once, the road signs speak Spanish and strings of red chiles decorate the doorways of the ubiquitous adobe haciendas. Here, Spanish, Mexican, Native American, and Anglo cultures have blended to form a unique society (and an unbeatable cuisine). Yet, each retains a sense of identity.

This is particularly so with the local Native Americans. Among the most traditional of all natives in North America are the Pueblo Indians. Divided into 19 groups, the Pueblos occupy the north-central and northwest portions of New Mexico, from Isleta, south of Albuquerque, to Taos in the north. Many of the sub-tribes have occupied their homelands continuously since before Europeans walked the American soil.

Several of the following adventures bring you in close contact with pueblos; to visit one is to step back in time. Not all permit visitors, and of those that do, most enforce stiff regulations concerning snapshot-taking and other matters of etiquette. You'll find the rules posted at the entrance to each.

Santa Fe

The most captivating community in the Land of Enchantment is beautiful—if somewhat trendy—Santa Fe, the oldest capital city in America. Strict building codes require adobe-style architecture, lending the city the appearance of a large pueblo.

The Palace of the Governors, built in 1610 (10 years before the Mayflower landed at Plymouth Rock), is the oldest continuously used

Enchanting Santa Fe

government building in the United States. It has housed the governments of five peoples: the Spanish, who built the palace; the Pueblos, who, following an uprising against the Spanish in the late 1600s, ruled Santa Fe for 12 years; and the Mexicans, Confederates, and Americans. In 1909 the prestigious Museum of New Mexico was started in the palace, and today it still serves as one unit of the four-facility complex. Occasionally during the year, Pueblo, Navajo, Hopi, and other Indians flock to town to sell pottery and jewelry, spreading their wares on woven blankets beneath the open-air portico of the palace.

Devote a day to pedaling around Santa Fe's old neighborhoods. Spin up Canyon Road and browse through a few of its myriad shops and galleries. It's said that Santa Fe is the heart of the Southwest and that Canyon Road is the soul of Santa Fe. A city bicycle map is available through the Transportation Planning Department, (505) 988-7433.

Ride 26 begins just a few blocks from the Old Santa Fe Plaza. If you turn left instead of right, seduced by the mesmerizing city and postponing your fat-tire visit to the surrounding Sangre de Cristo Mountains, who can blame you?

The supplemental map needed for Santa Fe and environs is the Santa Fe National Forest visitors map, available through the Forest Supervisor's Office, 1220 St. Francis Drive, Santa Fe, NM 87504, (505) 988-6940, and at district offices in Coyote, Cuba, Española, Los Alamos, Jemez Springs, Las Vegas, and Pecos.

26. Santa Fe Down

Riding surface:	Pavement, smooth dirt, single-track trail
Elevation range:	6,609 to 10,320 feet
Distance:	35 miles
Relative difficulty:	Hard
Time to allow:	5 to 9 hours
Best time of year:	June through October
Supplemental map:	Santa Fe National Forest visitors map

There aren't as many fillies and colts running along the Winsor Trail portion of this outing as at the world-famous Santa Fe Downs racetrack, but you might encounter a party or two of equestrians riding out of the historic Bishops Lodge. Ride sharp in the saddle, and be prepared to stop, dismount, and let the thoroughbreds walk safely by.

The ride, climbing 3,700 feet above Santa Fe, winds up the dirt road through Pacheco Canyon to the Santa Fe Ski Basin. From the ski area, you're faced with a choice: take the designated route that heads down Tesuque Creek along the fun and technically challenging Winsor Trail, or follow paved Hyde Park Road back to Santa Fe. Try to go on a weekday if you don't like traffic.

From the northeast corner of the plaza in Old Santa Fe, go north on Washington Street for 0.5 mile and cross Paseo de Peralta. Park just beyond, at the corner of Washington Street/Bishops Lodge Road and Artist Road/Hyde Park Road.

Go north on Washington Street, soon to become Bishops Lodge Road. Winding uphill on pavement through the Sangre de Cristo foothills, pass by numerous, picturesque adobe homes planted among the junipers and the piñons. At 2.0 crest a hill and coast down, passing the right-hand turn to Bishops Lodge at 2.9 miles.

The road narrows as it snakes through timbered bottomland. At 5.0 pass by a foundry/gallery with whimsical sculptures animating the grounds. At 5.5 go straight at the crossroads; at the stop sign in 0.1 mile turn right onto State Highway 591. Still in a rural residential area, enter the Tesuque Indian Reservation at 5.9 miles.

At 6.7 miles turn right onto State Highway 592 toward Rancho Encantado. At 7.1 pass County Road 74 on the right; continue straight, topping out at 7.4. At 8.7 enter the Rancho Encantado rural-home area, the last of the city and the beginning of *el campo*, the country.

At 10.1 miles go straight uphill onto gravel County Road 76, as the pavement curves left. Cross over a cattle guard onto USFS lands at

11.5, where the road becomes Forest Road 102. Continue up and down as the road becomes more primitive, passing by several cabins around 12.5 miles. You're now riding among stands of ponderosa pine, with large cottonwoods lining the riparian creek corridor.

Switching from one side of the creek to the other through a narrowing of rock outcrops, the climb is arduous at times. Turn right at the junction at 16.1, continuing steeply up Forest Road 102 as Forest Road 412 heads left toward Aspen Ranch.

At 17.5 miles the Winsor Trail—trail 254—bisects the road (you'll cross the road at this point on the trail at mile 24.2). At 18.3, where the grade relaxes a bit, you earn good views of the locally touted "world's largest aspen stand." Cross a cattle guard at 18.8 and turn left uphill onto pavement at 19.1.

On the right at 19.9 miles is Aspen Grove Picnic Ground. Top out at 20.9, approaching the Santa Fe Ski Basin. At 21.5 bear right, passing the Super Chief quad lift, and circle back. At 21.8 turn right toward the Winsor Trail; after crossing the small footbridge, turn left onto the Winsor Trail (right leads into the off-limits-to-bikes Pecos Wilderness.

(Note: for the road option, simply zip back down the paved Hyde Park Road for 14.6 miles to the corner of Washington Street and Artist Road, regained at 36.4 miles. En route you'll pass Big Tesuque Campground [at mile 24.7], Hyde State Park [28.0], a restaurant [29.1], Black Canyon Campground [29.4], and a commercial spa [33.0] replete with hot pools, cold plunges, saunas, massages, and herbal wraps.)

At 21.9 cross the creek on a plank bridge. Several rock and wood waterbars follow, so ride with care. At 22.0, immediately after passing through a fenceline, turn left following Trail 254 as Trail 163 goes right. Cross the creek, bearing left. At 22.1 miles pass through another fenceline, top out, and plunge down a 100-yard pitch.

Come to Hyde Park Road at 22.5 miles. Look for the Winsor Trail sign and follow it off the road down a steep embankment (do *not* bear right through the barriers onto the ski trails). At 22.8 miles pass through a gate, reclose it, and switchback right through a drainage, sidehilling through a stand of Douglas fir.

At 23.8 miles, among the quaking aspen, switchback right at the first in a series of eight hairpins. At 24.2 bear left onto Forest Road 102 for 50 feet, then drop onto Trail 254, following the sign reading "Bishops Lodge 6." In a small clearing at 24.7 miles bear right at the wooden post. Climb for 200 yards and resume coasting.

At 25.1 follow the sign directing you toward Bishops Lodge.

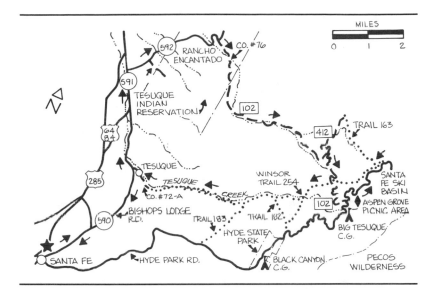

Continue straight at 26.0 as another trail veers to the left. At 26.8, where Trail 182 goes left, continue straight along the right side of the creek and begin sidehilling along a dry slope vegetated with yucca, sage, ponderosa pine, gambel oak, and mountain maple.

At 27.1, at a primitive campsite, swing left through the creek. At 27.7, continue straight as another trail goes left. At 28.1 climb temporarily above the creek, then squeeze into the dramatically narrowing canyon. Over the course of the next 2 miles, splash through Tesuque Creek 14 times, battling brush and rock the while. Prior to crossing number 15, at 30.2 miles, the trail broadens as it begins traversing a sunny, piñon-and-juniper-covered slope.

At 30.3 miles cross the log barrier and, rather than crossing the bridge onto the private property of the Bishops Lodge, ford the creek and follow the trail veering right along the stream corridor. At 30.5 turn left onto County Road 72-A, and pass through Tesuque. At 31.1 turn left onto Bishops Lodge Road/State Highway 590, closing the loop. Spin by Bishops Lodge at 32.1. At 35.0 miles you've successfully found your way back to the corner of Washington Street and Artist Road.

You're hot, tired, and thirsty. Do this: drag yourself the half-mile back into Old Sante Fe, sit down in the open-air patio of a restaurant, and enjoy some blue-corn tortilla enchiladas with posole and Hatch chiles, washed down with a cold *cerveza* (beer). *¡Con mucho gusto!*

Log flume, along the High Road to Taos

Taos

Taos Pueblo is the most renowned of the New Mexico pueblos. Four hundred years ago, the smooth-surfaced, golden-brown structures here led Spanish explorers to believe they had located one of the lost cities of gold. Now a national historic site, Taos Pueblo has been nominated to become the fifteenth American addition to crucial sites recognized by the World Heritage Commission. Perhaps the pueblo is, after all, worth its weight in gold.

Although many of its residents keep modern homes nearby—of the approximately 2,000 Indians living on the reservation, only 150 live full-time in the village itself—in the pueblo the houses have no electricity or plumbing. Water is retrieved from the Taos River, which divides the settlement in half.

The town of Taos, 2 miles south of the pueblo, is like a small version of Santa Fe. At hand are great eateries, top-notch galleries, fine accommodations, good bookstores and museums, and nearly any recreational diversion desired.

When traveling between Santa Fe and Taos, bypass the main highway and drive the High Road to Taos (also known as, not surprisingly, the High Road to Santa Fe). For 50 miles it dips and rises over pastoral, mountain-fringed countryside and leads through traditional villages like Truchas, Las Trampas, and Peñasco, site of the Picuris Pueblo. You'll see ancient churches, hollowed-out-log water flumes, tortillerias. The sweeping vistas and rolling nature of the highway make it a premier paved-road ride, and it also provides access to several potentially first-class mountain-bike adventures.

The supplemental map needed for Taos and the surrounding area is the Carson National Forest visitors map, available through the Forest Supervisor's Office, 208 Cruz Alta Road, Taos, NM 87571, (505) 758-6200, and at district offices in Canjilon, Abiquiu, El Rito, Blanco, Peñasco, Tres Piedras, and Questa.

27. Maestas Ridge Climb

Riding surface: Pavement, smooth and bumpy gravel road
Elevation range: 7,415 to 10,403 feet
Distance: 25.7 miles
Relative difficulty: Hard
Time to allow: 4 to 6 hours
Best time of year: June through October
Supplemental map: Carson National Forest visitors map

Eat your power-packed Super Crunchies before tackling this ride. It leads up an incredibly steep and seemingly endless hill. Along the way, long-range vistas are common, so there's always a good excuse for stopping to catch your breath and massage your quadriceps.

From Taos, go 3 miles south on State Highway 68 to Ranchos de Taos and turn left onto State Road 518, passing through Talpa. In 7

Rio Grande del Rancho

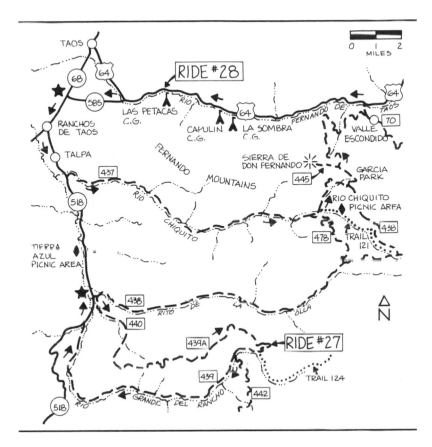

miles (roughly 2 miles south of Tierra Azul Picnic Area), park at the turnoff to Forest Road 438.

Pedal up Forest Road 438, turn right in 0.1 mile onto Forest Road 440, and progress upward toward Maestas Park through a forest of piñon, juniper, and ponderosa pine. Beyond the gate at 0.9 the road becomes steeper, narrower, rougher, and darker in color. Although the grade diminishes here and there, the majority of the next 6 miles is a steep uphill grind. En route, Forest Road 440M goes left at 2.4 miles, Forest Road 440I veers left at 4.7, Forest Road 440L goes left at 5.3, and Forest Road 440J heads left at 6.7. Near 7.0 miles, through the trees, you can spot the Taos valley in the distance.

Exhilarating, roller-coaster ridge riding leads to 10.5, where the route designation changes to Forest Road 439A. At 11.3, if you've come to what looks like a virtual *wall* in the road and find yourself asking, "How am I going to get up that?!" then you're at the right place. In

0.1 mile, at the ridgetop, curve right and continue along Forest Road 439A.

At 12.0 miles, where a track goes uphill to the left, continue on the level, bearing right. There's a lot of downhill ahead to make up for all the uphill behind: at 12.1 is the first in a series of three switchbacks. At the bottom of the hill, at 13.1, Cerro Vista Trail 124 goes left; you bear right downstream along Rio Grande del Rancho, also known as the Little Rio Grande (meaning, if translated entirely to English, "little big river"). An abundance of waterfalls and deep holes can be spotted along this stream, among the most popular fishing waters in the Taos area. At 14.1 miles, where Forest Road 442 goes left, continue straight on Forest Road 439. It's pretty tough to get lost over the next few miles: simply follow the main track as it alternates between smooth and rocky, up and down. Zip by some of the bluest blue spruce you'll ever see, as well as several nice primitive campsites.

Following 0.5 mile of easy uphill at 19.5, scream downhill. Pass a set of ponds near 22.5 miles, then cross the bridge spanning the river. At 24.0 miles continue on Forest Road 439, crossing a cattle guard at 24.5 then turning right onto State Road 518. Return to your point of departure at 25.7 miles.

That was a lot of work. Don't deprive yourself of a dip in the river or—back in civilized Taos—a dip in some salsa.

28. Rio Chiquito Bandito

Riding surface:	Pavement, smooth to rocky gravel surface
Elevation range:	6,952 to 10,064 feet
Distance:	37.2 miles
Relative difficulty:	Hard
Time to allow:	4 to 8 hours
Best time of year:	June through October
Supplemental map:	Carson National Forest visitors map

This outing encircles the Fernando Mountains, passing through some of the prettiest glades this side of *The Sound of Music*. It may steal your heart and never allow you to leave—in spirit, at least—the Land of Enchantment.

For several miles you parallel Rio Chiquito, a gurgling, picturesque mountain stream. Early in the day, mourning doves are cooing and flickers flicking about in the lush streamside vegetation. The path along the river is winding and its gradient ever-changing, creating extremely fun riding conditions. Many pleasant camping spots line the stream, so consider turning this one into an overnighter.

Toward the ride's end, 10 miles are along U.S. Highway 64. The highway carries less traffic during the week than on weekends. If, like some mountain bikers, you're allergic to highway riding, avoid it by shuttling a vehicle east of Taos to the junction of U.S. Highway 64 and Forest Road 70, at the sign pointing toward Valle Escondido.

Begin at the south end of Taos, at the junction of state highways 585 and 68, also known as the corner of Paseo del Pueblo Sur and Paseo de Cañon.

Pedal south on State Highway 68. At 1.4 miles turn left toward Peñasco onto State Highway 518, passing through Ranchos de Taos and Talpa. At 3.6 miles turn left onto Forest Road 437, leaving the pavement and heading up through the piñon and juniper. Cross a cattle guard at 4.2 and continue up, alongside thick, streamside vegetation.

At 6.8 the tight valley opens into meadows surrounded by stands of spruce and fir, with big hardwoods along the creek. Dozens of informal little campsites line this stretch of the creek. Ride over the creek on a bridge at 7.9 and climb steeply into a stand of ponderosa pine. Coast down and again cross the creek at 8.8 miles.

On the left at 9.6 are some beaver ponds; a little farther along the grade gets steeper. At 12.4 a primitive track goes right, down through the stream, as you continue up the main road. At 12.9, below on the right, is the beginning of a series of beaver ponds—look carefully and you'll spot a couple of active lodges—and falls along the creek. At 14.1 miles swing around the corner into a big meadow ringed with large aspen trees and, in their shade, shorter spruce trees.

At 14.5 bear straight/left uphill on Forest Road 437 as Forest Road 478 goes right. (Note: you can make a loop by following Forest Road 478 as it circles around to the south and joins Forest Road 438 going downstream along Rito de la Olla. It joins State Highway 518 at a point 5 miles south of where you left it, at mile 3.6.)

At 14.9 bear left on Forest Road 437, climbing steeply up Lagunita Canyon. (Note: at this point, Trail 121 goes right toward Rio Chiquito Picnic Area, a recommended base camp if you're interested in spending two or three days exploring in this area.) At 17.3 miles the grade subsides in a clearing as you parallel a fenceline on the left. At 17.4 fork left toward Garcia Park, following Forest Road 437, where Forest Road 438 goes toward Borrega Crossing.

Top out at 17.8 in Garcia Park and at 17.9 bear left, winding among stands of aspen. At 18.6 cross a cattle guard and go right at the fork, continuing on Forest Road 437 toward U.S. Highway 64, as primitive Forest Road 445 climbs to the left toward 10,365-foot Sierra de Don Fernando.

Start down at 18.7, careful not to run off the road while admiring the distant views. The road dips and rises and twists and turns as it loses elevation. Cross a cattle guard at 24.0, pass through a gate at 24.3, then merge left onto Forest Road 70. At 24.8 turn left onto U.S. Highway 64. The road hasn't much of a paved shoulder to offer, but it's fairly wide with generally adequate sight distances.

Pedaling along the pavement, note the dramatic contrast between the south- and north-facing slopes. The northern exposure provides shaded and damp growing conditions, encouraging heavy forest cover. In comparison, the sunny, desert-like southern slope is dotted with piñon and juniper.

On the left at 30.1 is La Sombra Campground and at 30.6 is Capulin Campground. At 33.3 pass Las Petacas Campground on the left. At 34.8 miles leave the Carson National Forest and in 0.25 mile turn left onto State Highway 585, a wide-shouldered and low-trafficked paved road heading through sage flats. From 35.5 it's generally downhill to the beginning point, reached at 37.2 miles.

Forest Road 437 winds down through spindly aspen forest.

29. Red River Valley

Riding surface: Gravel and dirt
Elevation range: 7,360 to 7,819 feet
Distance: 10.8 miles
Relative difficulty: Easy
Time to allow: 2 to 3 hours
Best time of year: May through November
Supplemental map: Carson National Forest visitors map

This ride offers views of, and an optional hike into, the valley of the Rio Grande, at the point where it accepts the waters of the Red River. At the confluence the gorge is more than 800 feet deep and a mile across. One of the first portions of river in America to be designated as such, the Rio Grande's "wild and scenic" stretch runs nearly 50 miles south from the Colorado border.

Cebolla Mesa Campground (USFS) is at mile 3.3 on the ride. You can use this primitive campground as a base (bring your own water) to explore the many gently graded paths in the vicinity. Or, stay at the undeveloped campsite where the ride dead-ends. A fragrant fire of sage and juniper, a twinkling night sky, and a dozen yipping coyotes will combine to put you in mind of the Sons of the Pioneers' cowboy tunes: "Tumbling Tumbleweed," "The Last Roundup," "Red River Valley." Don't forget to pack along your harmonica on this one.

Go 18 miles north of Taos on State Road 522, passing over high and dry sage-covered plateaus and dropping through lush, irrigated bottomlands. One-half mile past the Carson National Forest sign—immediately beyond milepost 15—turn left onto gravel Forest Road 9 and park at the first wide spot.

Begin winding westward, across terrain sprinkled with sage, piñon, and juniper. In the distance is the gorge of the Rio Grande. Here and there along the way, primitive paths fork left or right; stick to the primary track.

At 0.6 bottom out in a draw where Forest Road 483 goes right; start up and then pass under and begin paralleling a power line. At 1.0, at the Cebolla Mesa sign, curve right away from the power line. Go down, hitting bottom at 1.7 miles. Steal a glimpse of the abrupt mountain front behind you—it's a beauty.

Curve right at 1.9 where Forest Road 483 forks left (another path worthy of exploring, it traces Garrapata Ridge). Pass through a gate at 3.0 and coast by some old corrals on the left at 3.2 miles. Enter the campground circle at 3.3 miles; after peeking over the rim and exclaiming, "Oooooaaaaahhhhh," bear right on what initially appears to be a

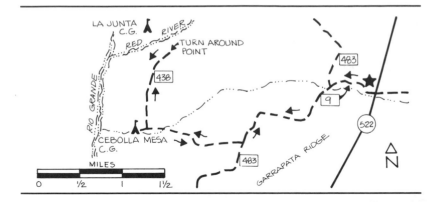

continuation of the main road. It deteriorates delightfully once out of the camping area, as it runs along the flats back from the rim.

At 4.5 curve left to parallel the fenceline, and at 4.7 cross a cattle guard onto Forest Road 438. At 4.9 zip down through an eroded draw and begin up, continuing straight at the top rather than bearing right. At 5.2 turn left and cross a washout; in 0.25 mile the path dead-ends at a terrific little pine-studded, boulder-protected campsite.

Ahead is the gorge of the Red River, formed by the river carving its way down to the level of the Rio Grande. Beyond, on the rim across the gorge, you can spot La Junta Campground—not far as the buzzard flies, but you can't get there from here! (Note: slated for the not-too-distant future is construction of a bridge spanning the gorge, connecting La Junta Point and the Cebolla Mesa Trail. The U.S. Air Force has offered helicopters to airlift the bridge into position.)

Jemez Mountains

New Mexico's very best mountain-bike riding may be that lying within the Jemez Mountains and along the adjacent Pajarito Plateau's finger-like mesas and water-carved canyons. The range encircles the Valle Grande Caldera, one of the world's largest extinct volcanic craters. The rim of the crater can be envisioned when gazing at the ring of ridges and peaks surrounding the caldera—consider this when relishing the views from atop Cerro Pelado (ride 32).

The caldera, 16 miles across, lies largely within the 100,000-acre Baca Location 1, a massive private holding that interrupts the continuity of the mountains' USFS lands and eliminates the legality of several intriguing mountain-bike loops.

The Bandelier Tuff that forms the honeycombed cliffs in this country is comprised of ash, compressed and hardened over time, that piled up during the big volcano's violent long-ago eruptions. Naturally occurring caves in the soft tuff—sometimes excavated to make them larger and more livable—provided homes to some of the first Anasazis ("ancient ones") to wander into the region.

Several Indian pueblos lie at the southern edge of the Jemez Mountains, including the Jemez, Santo Domingo, and Cochiti pueblos. The setting for N. Scott Momaday's 1969 Pulitzer Prize-winning *House Made of Dawn* is Cañon de San Diego, the valley that the town of Jemez Springs sits in. To read this novel is to develop a sense of the magic, mystery, and Indian lore that await your discovery in the beautiful Jemez Mountains.

Incongruously situated amidst the peaceful, natural setting of the mountain range is bustling Los Alamos, birthplace of the atomic bomb. If you happen to be driving along either State Highway 4 or State Highway 30 east of Los Alamos at rush hour, you'll suspect that half the population of New Mexico works in the nearby nuclear-testing facilities. The daily, L.A.-style traffic jams seem very much out of place in the rural mountain setting.

The supplemental map needed for the Jemez Mountains is the Santa Fe National Forest visitors map, available through the Forest Supervisor's Office, 1220 St. Francis Drive, Santa Fe, NM 87504, (505) 988-6940, and at district offices in Coyote, Cuba, Española, Los Alamos, Jemez Springs, Las Vegas, and Pecos.

30. Cochiti Splash

Riding surface:	Smooth to rocky gravel surface
Elevation range:	6,000 to 7,360 feet
Distance:	14.4 miles
Relative difficulty:	Easy
Time to allow:	2 to 5 hours
Best time of year:	April through November
Supplemental map:	Santa Fe National Forest visitors map

If it's a hot summer's day, do this ride—the many creek crossings and the shade provided by ancient ponderosa pines will combine to keep you cool. If it's not hot, do it anyway. This round trip through the narrow and scenic canyon lets you splash through Cochiti Creek a remarkable 50 times. If you're not grinning ear-to-ear during and after this ride, then your mouth won't bend that way. Dozens of inviting primitive campsites line the length of the canyon.

Getting to this ride's beginning point is trickier than finding your way once the riding commences. From Interstate 25, between Santa Fe

Save the past for the future

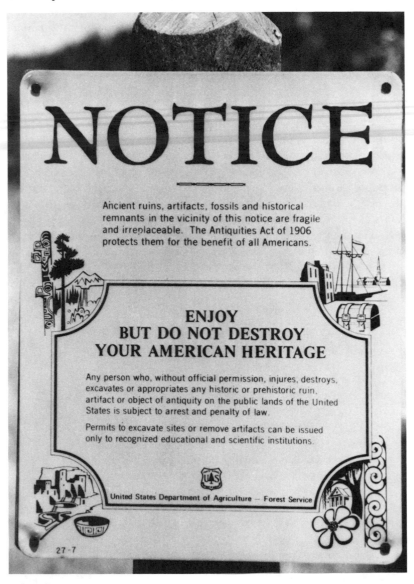

and Albuquerque, head north along State Highway 22 toward Santo Domingo Pueblo. After 11 miles pass through the town of Cochiti Lake. (The services here, including the local golf course, are operated by natives of nearby Cochiti Pueblo.) Three miles north of town, the road becomes gravel. One-and-a-quarter miles after entering Rancho de la Cañada, where the main road (Forest Road 268) goes left, continue straight ahead on Forest Road 89. In 0.5 mile, enter the Dixon Apple Orchard, skirting a work-of-art river-cobble fence and heeding the sign warning that "Apple eaters have right-of-way." Pass by the ranch headquarters in another 0.5 mile, then cross a cattle guard onto USFS lands.

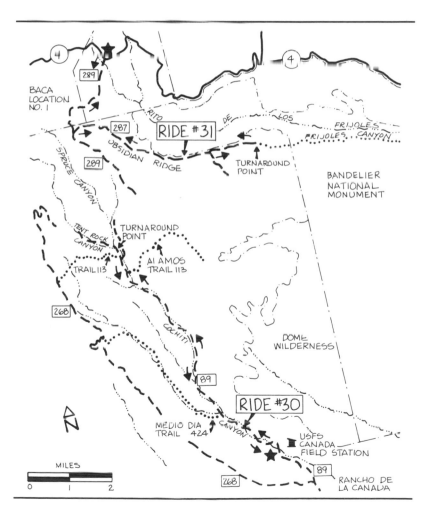

Immediately after going over a bridge, bear right and park near the out-houses.

Pedal up Forest Road 89, disregarding the sign warning "Dead end road—not maintained." (Translated, this simply means that it's a road that is terrible for cars but terrific for mountain bikes.) Start climbing and curve left away from the adobe structure housing the USFS Cañada Field Station.

As you rise above the canyon, cliffs of porous Bandelier Tuff pop into view; scan them and look for raptors, swallows, and swifts. Behind in the distance are the Sandia Peaks, which border Albuquerque on the east. Begin coasting into the canyon at 1.2, and at 1.4 miles splash through the first of many creek crossings, some much deeper than others, as your feet soon will attest. Pass by a cabin and across a short stretch of private land at 2.1 miles; at 2.2 Medio Dia Trail 424 goes left.

At 5.1 miles, at what would have been the thirteenth pass through Cochiti Creek, the road engineer had a bridge built over the stream. Why, when the 25 other crossings were left unbridged, is one of the not-so-ancient mysteries of the Jemez Mountains.

Continuing upstream and getting wetter and wetter, at 6.8 Alamos Trail 113 veers to the right. At 7.2 bear left uphill; the right fork goes through a gate, up Spruce Canyon for 1 mile, and then dead-ends. At 7.3, go straight toward Pines as Trail 113 goes left and begins climbing onto Cochiti Mesa. Turn around at the gate at 7.4 miles, beyond which the road enters private land, and splish-splash your way back to where you started.

(Note: continuing across the private land, the road penetrates Tent Rock Canyon. By checking first with Santa Fe National Forest personnel, you may be able to obtain permission to pedal to the volcanic landscape.)

31. Bandelier Tough

Riding surface:	Smooth gravel, rutted dirt
Elevation range:	7,990 to 8,949 feet
Distance:	15.4 miles
Relative difficulty:	Moderate
Time to allow:	2 to 4 hours
Best time of year:	May through October
Supplemental map:	Santa Fe National Forest visitors map

On this ride you look down from Obsidian Ridge into the canyon of El Rito de Frijoles. Note on the forest visitors map that, along Obsidian Ridge, you're only a couple of ridges east of Cochiti Canyon (ride 30); however, the ridgetop environment is a different world altogether from the riparian canyon.

Adolph Bandelier, the prominent late-nineteenth-century Swiss archaeologist/explorer, spent a decade among the Pueblo Indians of New Mexico. Although Frijoles Canyon was deserted before the Spanish arrived, Bandelier was convinced that it was Indians ancestral to those of the Cochiti Pueblo who settled there, enlarging natural caves in the volcanic tuff and building adobe structures for shelter.

You can see the cave shelters and the reconstructed village today at Bandelier National Monument. Besides offering a fine museum and living-prehistory exhibit, the monument encompasses more than 20,000 acres of little-visited wilderness. You can't mountain-bike there, but feel free to poke around on foot and see some amazing things.

In his entertaining and painstakingly accurate novel of prehistory, *The Delight Makers*, Bandelier reconstructed daily life in "the Rito." It's not difficult to imagine one of the book's characters, on a summer day, climbing out of the Rito and up onto Obsidian Ridge, searching for the raw materials to fashion spear points from. To camp out on the ridge at the turnaround point and gaze out over the Rito, the Pajarito Plateau, and the broad basin beyond would be a mystical experience. But pick your night carefully, for it also could be an electrifying experience. If thunderstorms threaten, opt instead for the developed campground in Bandelier National Monument.

From the entrance to Bandelier National Monument, proceed northwest along wildly winding State Highway 4 as it follows the monument's northern boundary. In about 12 miles, before leaving the national monument, turn left onto Forest Road 289 and park at the first wide spot.

Pedal southward through Bandelier National Monument on high-grade Forest Road 289. At 1.2 leave the monument and cut through a corner of Baca Location 1 on the public-access road. At 2.1 miles enter the Santa Fe National Forest, coast down to 2.2, and turn left onto Forest Road 287.

Bear straight at 2.3 where Forest Road 2480 goes left, and start down through the forest of pine, spruce, and aspen. Hit bottom at 2.7 and start up, passing through a gate. At 3.0 curve right on the similar-surfaced road as a primitive road forks left. As the timber cover thins out, long-range views begin to appear.

Go through a gate at 4.5 miles and start down along a rougher surface. The boundary of Bandelier National Monument is immediately on the left as you bump down the knife-edge ridge. Bottom out at 5.2 where the path enters a young tree plantation in this burned-over area. The country opens dramatically and the road is quite rutted in places.

Keep an eye out for wild raspberries, abundant since wildfire raged through in 1977.

At 6.5 miles bear left on the main fork. At the edge of the ridge at 7.7 you encounter a series of "Kelly humps," designed to close the road to further vehicular intrusion. The view from the turnaround point—into Frijoles Canyon and the Bandelier Wilderness and beyond to the populated valleys—is a vista worth holding onto for a while.

32. Cerro Pelado Hill Climb

Riding surface:	Smooth to rocky dirt and gravel
Elevation range:	8,151 to 10,109 feet
Distance:	23.8 miles
Relative difficulty:	Moderate
Time to allow:	3 to 5 hours
Best time of year:	May through October
Supplemental map:	Santa Fe National Forest visitors map

On a crystal New Mexico day, you can see forever from atop Cerro Pelado (bald mountain). To the north, within the Valle Grande Caldera, is Redondo Peak, a now-dormant volcano that sprang up during resurgence of the crater's floor. To the west, across Cañon de San Diego, is the Virgin Mesa. Farther in the distance, the Sangre de Cristos rise above Santa Fe and the Sandia Peaks above Albuquerque. On the clearest of days you can make out Mount Taylor, way to the west near the town of Grants.

Recommended base camps include Redondo Campground (USFS), 2 miles east of the junction of state highways 4 and 126, and the youth hostel located in Jemez Springs, 8 miles south of the junction. Also in Jemez Springs, and worthy of a post-ride visit, is a bathhouse/massage business.

From Redondo Campground go 4.8 miles east and turn south onto Forest Road 10 toward Ponderosa, and park at the first wide spot.

Pedal south down Forest Road 10 through the Vallecitos de los Indios rural residential area. At 0.5 mile cross a drainage and start gradually up, always bearing straight ahead rather than angling up the occasional driveway. At 1.5 miles pass through a gate onto USFS lands and climb beneath the forest cover of pine, spruce, and aspen.

Cerro Pelado Lookout offers one of New Mexico's grandest vistas.

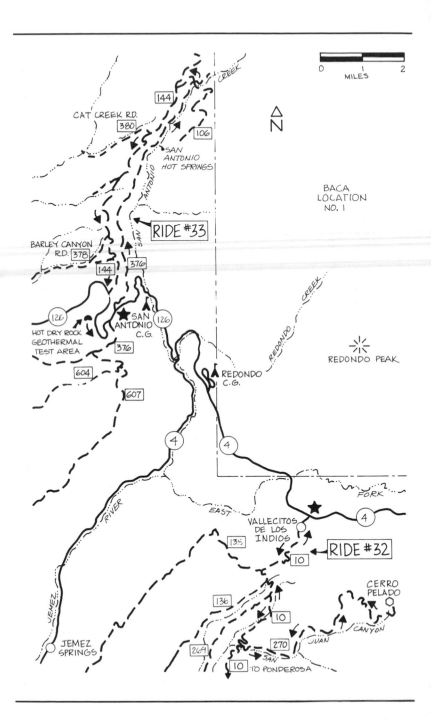

CREEK

144

CAT CREEK RD.
380

106

SAN
ANTONIO
HOT SPRINGS

N

BACA
LOCATION
NO. 1

RIDE #33

BARLEY CANYON
RD. 378

144   376

126

HOT DRY ROCK
GEOTHERMAL
TEST AREA

SAN
ANTONIO
C.G.

126

376

604

607

REDONDO
C.G.

REDONDO CREEK

REDONDO PEAK

4

4

RIVER

EAST

FORK

4

VALLECITOS
DE LOS
INDIOS

RIDE #32

135

10

CERRO
PELADO

JEMEZ

136

10

CANYON

JUAN

JEMEZ
SPRINGS

269

270

SAN

10 TO PONDEROSA

Continue straight on Forest Road 10 at 2.3. (Note: Forest Road 135, heading to the right, offers an intriguing ride along Cat Mesa. It degenerates into a four-wheel-drive track and exits the wilds approximately 16 miles to the south, on State Highway 290 near Ponderosa.)

As primitive Forest Road 136 goes right at 2.6, continue straight on Forest Road 10. Bottom out at 3.0 and at 3.1 continue straight on Forest Road 10 where Forest Road 269 goes right. At 5.4 miles turn left uphill onto Forest Road 270, leaving Forest Road 10 to its downhill run. For the next 2 miles the climb up San Juan Canyon is relatively gradual. Along the way you pass through meadows hiding several pleasant, primitive campsites.

After crossing a cattle guard at 7.3, the climbing intensifies; continue on the main track wherever a primitive path forks away. At 11.0 the steepness and rockiness may necessitate occasional walking. At 11.6 swing left and ride along the ridge to the lookout, gained at 11.9 miles. The lookout may or may not be manned; if it is, the person on duty may or may not invite you up. One way or the other, the views are stupendous. Backtrack to the beginning point at 23.8, being surprised at the 3-mile climb near the ride's end. And you thought it was all downhill from the lookout!

33. San Antonio Stroll

Riding surface:	Pavement, dirt/gravel
Elevation range:	8,250 to 8,840 feet
Distance:	16.1 miles
Relative difficulty:	Easy
Time to allow:	2 to 5 hours
Best time of year:	May through October
Supplemental map:	Santa Fe National Forest visitors map

After witnessing the lush countryside this route explores, you'll be convinced that portions of arid New Mexico's Jemez Mountains truly do receive 40-plus inches of precipitation a year. And that the mountains are a "hotbed" of subterranean activity is reinforced by the presence of the U.S. Government's Hot Dry Rock Geothermal Test Area, encountered along the State Highway 126 stretch of the ride.

You can base out of San Antonio Campground (USFS), situated beside State Highway 126 about 2 miles north of its junction with State Highway 4. The youth hostel in Jemez Springs, 8 miles south of the junction, is another good choice.

Along San Antonio Creek, in the Jemez Mountains

From San Antonio Campground, go 2.2 miles west and turn north onto Forest Road 376; park at the first wide shoulder.

Spin north along Forest Road 376. At 0.3 mile go down for a short distance, then head up through thick forest, topping out at 1.4. From this point, it's gradually down to 2.4 miles.

Continue up and down for the next couple of miles, at 4.6 skirting a stretch of cliffs. At 4.9, across the creek on the right, are the San Antonio Youth Conservation Corps camp and San Antonio Hot Springs, steam rising as the hot water flows over rock. On a red-colored road surface, rise above open meadow rimmed in by cliffs, aspen groves, and verdant stands of spruce.

At 5.2 drop to creek level, then climb gradually to 5.9 miles. At 6.8 turn left up the big, steep hill as Forest Road 106 curves right. At 7.0 curve left; the grade intensifies for 0.5 mile. Pass through a gate at

7.5 and at the T in 0.1 mile turn left onto Forest Road 144. Commence pedaling on rolling ridgetop along the narrow road.

At 8.7 Cat Creek Road/Forest Road 380 goes right; continue straight uphill through evidence of recent logging. Topping out at 9.8, take a break from the saddle to walk over to the edge of the cliff on your left. Look down to where you were riding earlier, now just a stone's drop away.

Cross a cattle guard at 10.2 and then zip by a gated road heading right at 10.4 miles. At 12.1 Barley Canyon Road/Forest Road 378 veers right toward Fenton Lake. At 12.8 another road goes right as you continue straight. At 14.2 miles cross a cattle guard and turn left uphill onto State Highway 126, viewing Redondo Peak to the left. Just beyond the Hot Dry Rock Geothermal Test Area, on your right at 15.0, begin coasting back to the beginning point, reached at 16.1 miles.

Brazos and Tusas Mountains

Eastern gateway to the Brazos and Tusas mountains is the little truck-stop town of Tres Piedras; the quartzitic Brazos Cliffs give rise to the mountains on the west. Running north to the Colorado border, this portion of the Tres Piedras Ranger District hides some of the best and most remote mountain biking in the Four Corners Region.

The supplemental map needed for the Jemez Mountains is the Carson National Forest visitors map, available through the Forest Supervisor's Office, 208 Cruz Alta Road, Taos, NM 87571, (505) 758-6200, and at district offices in Canjillon, Abiquiu, El Rito, Blanco, Peñasco, Tres Piedras, and Questa.

34. Spring Creek Cruise

Riding surface: Pavement, gravel, rough dirt
Elevation range: 8,269 to 9,750 feet
Distance: 20.2 miles
Relative difficulty: Moderate
Time to allow: 3 to 5 hours
Best time of year: May through October
Supplemental map: Carson National Forest visitors map

You may want to consider combining rides 34 and 35 into one long loop of about 36 miles. And several other variations are possible by making the most of the area's extensive road system. Study the forest visitors map for a while and devise a personalized route—it's bound to be a good one, and you'll likely be the first to ride it.

From Tres Piedras, go approximately 7 miles west on U.S. Highway 64. Turn left onto gravel Forest Road 42, toward Cañon Plaza and Vallecitos, and park.

Pedal up Forest Road 42, first crossing a bridge at 0.2, then hooking sharp left at 0.4 mile. After a stretch of roller-coaster riding, at 1.6 miles pass through a fenceline and start up onto USFS lands. At 2.2 curve left through the draw, then swing right to begin a tough climb.

Top out on a cliffside at 3.3 and meet with a gasp-guaranteed view down into the wooded valley and Tusas Box Canyon. Wind, twist, and turn down the outrageous road, reaching bottom and curving left at 4.3 miles. In this wet riparian zone, big willows, aspen, and spruce tower above.

At 4.7 begin skirting a stretch of rock outcrops leading to a junction; turn right here onto Forest Road 91B toward Hopewell Lake. On

Deserted ranch, upper Spring Creek

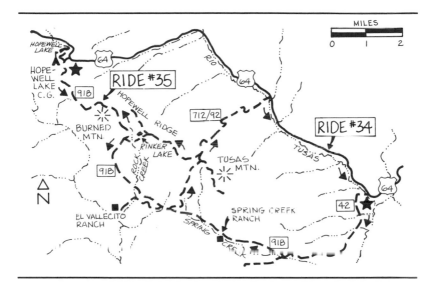

the smooth road, penetrate the picturesque valley of Spring Creek. Isolated Spring Creek Ranch is on the left at 6.4. At 7.8 miles pass by some old corrals and a dilapidated cabin, then begin climbing a steeper pitch.

At 8.7 miles pass over a cattle guard in open meadow; 0.25 mile beyond, turn right onto an unsigned road leading up through the meadow. (Note: if you come to a left-hand turn to El Vallecito Ranch, you've gone 0.1 mile too far.) The road turns steep and rocky. Cross a cattle guard at 9.2, after which the grade lessens. At 9.7 curve right around the head of a draw and continue up.

At 10.3 go straight as another path forks right. Arrive at the top at 10.4 miles and proceed along the ridge, passing a snow-survey marker on the right at 10.7 miles. At 11.1 come to a fenceline and continue straight, keeping it along your left side. Turn left at the fork at 11.4, where a right turn leads toward Tusas Mountain. At another fork at 11.8 bear right along Forest Road 712/92 toward U.S. Highway 64 (the left-hand road goes toward Burned Mountain).

Head down the high-grade road, winding through a series of S-turns during the first couple of miles. After 3 miles, break out into meadowland and cross a cattle guard at 14.8. At 15.5 turn right onto U.S. Highway 64 and spin smoothly along paved shoulder for 4.5 miles as the highway traces the wide-open, mountain-ringed valley. Return to your beginning point at 20.2.

35. Hopewell Ridge Loop

Riding surface: Smooth gravel, rough dirt
Elevation range: 9,061 to 10,010 feet
Distance: 18.7 miles
Relative difficulty: Moderate
Time to allow: 3 to 5 hours
Best time of year: May through October
Supplemental map: Carson National Forest visitors map

The soft and rolling countryside surrounding Hopewell Lake resulted from glaciers that moved through during the Pleistocene Ice Age. Sculpturing the landscape as they went, the rivers of ice carved a terrain ideal for fat-tire frolicking—let's hear it for glaciers!

The semi-primitive USFS campground (running water but no flush toilets) on the shores of Hopewell Lake serves as a fine base camp. On this outing keep a watch for the wild wapiti and mule deer abundant in the area.

From Tres Piedras, go about 20 miles west on U.S. Highway 64; turn left toward Hopewell Lake and park.

From its junction with U.S. Highway 64, ride south up Forest Road 91B, passing the right-hand turn into Hopewell Lake Campground at 0.2 mile. After a brisk downhill, cross through a flat and wet meadow at 2.3 and start climbing. The hill crests at 3.3 miles, not far below the 10,189-foot peak of Burned Mountain.

Coast down, quite steeply at times, through meadow and forest. At 7.0 miles—about the time you begin to think, "I'm in trouble; I've lost a heckuva lot more elevation than I've gained!"—you cross Rock Creek and begin repaying your elevation debt.

At 8.2 miles pass the road going right into El Vallecito Ranch. In 0.1 mile, turn left onto a primitive, unsigned path leading through a cow pasture; it quickly becomes quite steep and rocky. (Note: the next 2.9 miles are coincidental with mile 8.9 through 11.8 on ride 34.) Cross over a cattle guard at 8.6, after which the grade diminishes. At 9.1 curve right around the head of a draw and continue up.

At 9.7 go straight as another path forks right. Arrive at the top of the climb at 9.8, then enjoy a stretch of quick ridgetop riding, passing a snow-survey marker on your right at 10.1 miles. At 10.5 continue straight, keeping the fenceline to your left. Turn left at 10.8, where the right fork leads to Tusas Mountain. At a second fork at 11.2, turn left toward Burned Mountain (the other option follows Forest Road 712/92 to U.S. Highway 64, where you would turn left).

Top out on Hopewell Ridge at 11.7 and zip down to 12.1, where the grade diminishes. Continue on the main road as primitive paths fork left at 12.3 and right at 12.4 miles. The road soon begins deteriorating as it winds amidst forest and through meadow. At 13.4 miles, where the road levels off, turn left at the fork. Don't miss this turn—going to the right will drop you into never-never land!

Tiny Rinker Lake is on the right at 13.5. Coast down through the Rock Creek drainage at 13.9, then climb to 14.1 miles and turn right onto Forest Road 91B, closing the loop. It's a steep grunt back up to Burned Mountain summit at 15.4 miles. Continue retracing your tracks to the ride's beginning, reached at 18.7 miles.

Other Rides in New Mexico

By now, you agree that some of the West's best fat-tire flying is found in the Land of Enchantment. Scores of other areas in the northwest and north-central portions of the state are worthy of exploring.

Santa Fe National Forest. On Santa Fe National Forest lands, sample some of the many dirt paths forking off State Highway 63 as it forges north from Pecos National Monument and follows the valley of the Pecos River into the mountains. Suggestions: Forest Road 123, heading into Dalton Canyon; Forest Road 122, which follows Holy Ghost Creek to the boundary of the Pecos Wilderness; and Forest Road 645, as it climbs to the east toward 11,659-foot Elk Mountain.

Miles of intriguing dirt roads bisect Glorieta Mesa, south of Pecos. The best access to the mesa is provided by State Highway 34, as it runs south from Interstate 25.

From Abiquiu, the late Georgia O'Keeffe's home, go west on U.S. Highway 84 and State Highway 96 to the town of Gallina. From there, drive to the north and east on Forest Road 8 and on Forest Road 77. Then snoop out some of the primitive roads looping onto the series of mesas that skirt the Chama River Wilderness and overlook the Rio Chama. You could easily spend a week exploring this portion of the Santa Fe National Forest.

Beginning immediately across the highway from the departure point for the San Antonio Stroll (ride 33) is another first-class outing. Follow Forest Road 376 to the south, turning left onto Forest Road 604 after 1.25 miles. In another 1.25 miles, turn left onto Forest Road 607. This by-way leads out along Virgin Mesa and provides views into Cañon de San Diego. Approximately 10 miles after leaving Forest Road 376, at a scattering of old log buildings, turn west onto the faint path and continue for a few hundred yards. Here, overlooking Jemez Springs, you'll spot some large mounds—the ruins of a prehistoric pueblo. Like all ruins, these are protected by federal law, so don't disturb them.

Taos. If you want some additional rides while in Taos, a few options include La Jara Canyon, the Ojitos Trail, Gallegos Peak, Picuris Peak, and the Devisadero Loop Trail. For more details, pick up the *Mountain Cycling* brochure, available at the local USFS office.

Rio Chama. A route traversing lands administered by both the Carson and the Santa Fe national forests begins along U.S. Highway 84, approximately 17 miles north of Abiquiu. One mile north of the turnoff to the fascinating USFS-operated Ghost Ranch Living Museum, turn left onto Forest Road 151 and begin cruising. After leading 5 miles to the southwest, the gravel road runs into the Rio Chama and bends to wind along its north bank. The gorgeous canyon defines a gap in the Chama River Wilderness; while pedaling through it you're completely surrounded by, but outside of, the wilderness area.

After roughly 9 miles of riverside riding, the route dead-ends at the Church of the Desert, a monastery inhabited by several monks. Use the Carson National Forest visitors map for this ride, an outing that provides plenty of opportunities to go for a cooling dip.

Rio Puerco Resource Area. The Rio Puerco Resource Area of the BLM administers more than 1 million acres of northwest New Mexico lands, mostly in the Albuquerque, Grants, and Cuba vicinities. It's predominantly low-lying, arid land and not the lovely timbered-mountain settings more typical of the lands administered by the USFS in New Mexico. However, terrific rides can be found on BLM lands, in areas ordinarily not frequented by hordes of other recreationists.

East of San Ysidro, at the southwest end of the Jemez Mountains, two geographical features—El Cabezon and Ojito, each encompassing a Wilderness Study Area (WSA)—come highly recommended.

El Cabezon is the largest of several dozen basaltic volcanic necks existing in the area. The primitive roads surrounding its base traverse grassy foothills and cross the many arroyos that occasionally carry water down from the 7,785-foot peak. To get there, drive 20 miles north of San Ysidro on State Highway 44 and turn south onto County Road 279. After passing through the village of San Luis, it's 10 miles to the northwest boundary of the WSA and the privately owned ghost town of Cabezon.

Beginning near the bridge crossing, ride 6 miles south along the western boundary of the WSA, then 5 miles on a rough dirt road along the southern boundary. Great views into the Rio Puerco Valley are gained along this stretch. Go north for 5 miles and turn onto the pipeline road, following it north for 3 miles, back to County Road 279 and a fording of the Rio Puerco River. (By turning south rather than north onto the pipeline road, you'll reach Ojito WSA in 11 miles.) It's then 3 miles back to the beginning point, for a total loop distance of 22 miles.

At Ojito, a natural area and WSA encompassing more than 10,000 acres, sedimentary rocks have been carved into badland canyons, high cliffs, and eerie sculptures. From 2 miles south of San Ysidro on State Highway 44, pedal south and west for several miles on a maintained dirt road; en route you'll begin skirting the WSA boundary. After about 11 miles, turn around and backtrack. Or, turn northwest onto the pipeline road, which provides splendid views as it leads the 11 miles to the Cabezon WSA boundary.

Another good ride is the route to and through the Tent Rocks Special Management Area (SMA). The odd, tent-shaped erosional remnants, comprised of volcanic pumice and tuff, have formed courtesy of the protection provided by their erosion-resistant caprocks.

Begin by following the directions leading to Cochiti Splash (ride 30). Once across the dam spanning the Rio Grande, turn left toward Cochiti Pueblo. In 1.5 miles, park at the brightly colored water tower and begin riding by turning right onto graded-dirt Road 266. It's 3 miles to the boundary of the SMA, then another 4 miles to USFS lands. Backtrack, for a round-trip distance of 14 miles, or continue to Jemez Pueblo and State Highway 4, approximately 25 hilly miles beyond.

Maps and additional information on Cabezon, Ojito, and Tent Rocks SMA can be obtained by contacting the BLM's Rio Puerco Resource Area, 435 Montano Northeast, Albuquerque, NM 87107.

El Malpais National Conservation area. Among the most impressive displays of volcanism in the Southwest is El Malpais (the badlands), an expansive lava field encompassing an array of natural phenomena including cinder cones, lava tubes, ice caves, sandstone formations, and pine forests. Through an act of Congress in 1987 the natural area became El Malpais National Monument. Although the heart of the area is now administered by the National Park Service and is off-limits to bicycle travel, you can cycle through the surrounding El Malpais National Conservation Area, managed by the BLM.

A suggested tour begins at the junction of State Highway 53 and County Road 42, roughly 25 miles south of Grants on State Highway 53. Starting near Bandera Crater, the largest of several cinder cones in El Malpais, the 35-mile ride follows County Road 42 as it skirts the boundary of the West Malpais Wilderness. The road traverses hardened lava flows that have periodically poured out over the McCarty Valley during the past 3,000 years.

Nearing the Continental Divide crossing, spread out before you is a line of 30 cinder cones in the Chain of Craters WSA. After 35 miles, the road runs into State Highway 117; from here you must either backtrack, complete a huge circle, or take advantage of your wise decision to have shuttled a vehicle to this point.

For more details, contact the BLM/NPS El Malpais Information Center, 620 East Santa Fe Street, Grants, NM 87020.

Grants. Also near Grants, the Mount Taylor Ranger District personnel know of miles of roads to recommend that provide scenic riding in the vicinity of Mount Taylor, northeast of Grants, and in the Zuni Mountains, southwest of town. For maps and information, contact the Cibola National Forest, Mount Taylor Ranger District, 1800 Lobo Canyon Road, Grants, NM 87020.

Albuquerque. Near Albuquerque, check out the Cedro Peak Area, 15 miles from the city. To get there, head east on Interstate 40 and turn south at Tijeras, following winding State Highway 337. In 5 miles, turn east onto Forest Road 242. This leads to a camping/parking area where several loops begin that follow dirt roads and trails. For both the area USFS visitors map and for a sketch map of the designated mountain-bike trails, contact the Cibola National Forest, Sandia Ranger District, 11776 Highway 337 South, Tijeras, NM 87059.

Limited but spectacular riding options can be found adjacent to the Sandia Crest National Scenic Byway, just east of the Sandia Mountain Wilderness. This area also is depicted on the Sandia Ranger District visitors map.

Farmington. Near Farmington, in the extreme northwest corner of New Mexico, try out the Glade Run Trail System, a 40-mile network of old roads and trails just north of town. The system is managed specifically for mountain bikes and small ORVs. Trails wind through rolling piñon-juniper woodlands and sage flats.

The Angel Peak Recreation Area, 35 miles southeast of Farmington, offers miles of old oil and gas roads traversing a landscape of badlands. The Spaniards called Angel Peak *nacimiento* ("birthplace") and to the Navajos it was a dwelling place of their sacred ones.

For information on these areas, contact the BLM's Farmington Resource Area, Caller Service 4104, Farmington, NM 87499.

4
UTAH

According to Bicycle Utah, a non-profit group that is partly funded by the state travel council, Utah is the "Bicycle Capital of the United States." This ambitious claim is grounded in the Beehive State's vast and varied mountain-biking opportunities.

Like swallows to Capistrano, every spring thousands of mountain bikers flock to Moab, lending credence to Bicycle Utah's proclamation. But far fewer cyclists visit the outlying areas. Moab *is* special, but you could stand nearly anywhere in the southeastern quadrant of Utah and shoot an arrow into the air, and it would probably land on or near a terrific mountain-biking route.

Many first-class high-altitude routes are located in southeast

A sandy stretch of road winding amidst sandstone outcroppings

Utah, but the state's extra-special attraction—the one that draws the cycling hordes out of the winter woodwork—is the fabulous riding found
in and along its low-lying canyons and plateaus. Therefore, all of the
featured rides are of the desert, rather than the alpine, variety. For tips
on summer rides in the La Sals, Abajos, Henrys, and other mountain
ranges, see "Other Rides in Utah," at the end of the section.

Southeast Utah encompasses a lot of remote country and long,
empty stretches of road. Always leave town with a full tank of gas and
plenty of water and other supplies. If you find yourself wondering why
you drove 200 miles for *one* 15-mile ride, simply look around a bit.
Other great rides are probably close at hand, awaiting discovery.

Although not detailed enough to use for navigation, an excellent
overview map to carry when traveling here is the "Southeastern Utah
Multipurpose Map," available through the Utah Travel Council, Council Hall/Capitol Hill, Salt Lake City, UT 84114. One of a series of five
maps covering the entire state, it can't be beat as an aid to help you locate additional adventures.

Moab

Moab, once known as "the toughest town in Utah," mellowed
considerably after tourists supplanted cows and uranium as the driving
economic force. On the streets of Moab today, loud Lycra shorts are
more common than hard hats, and fat-tire bikes seemingly outnumber
horses 10,000 to one.

Moab has become to mountain biking what Aspen is to skiing: it
offers terrific riding along with a measure of fat-tire glitter. The 10.3-
mile Slickrock Bike Trail, initially responsible for Moab's preeminence
in the mountain-biking world, continues to be its most popular draw.
The trail has turned into a sort of Fort Lauderdale Beach of the desert—
visit it on a weekend during the spring-break season and you'll see bush
camps erected in every available nook and cranny of the frozen-dune
Navajo Sandstone, hear boom boxes blasting the blues, and find literally hundreds of cyclists.

Laid out on Bureau of Land Management lands in 1969 as a challenge for trail bikers, today the Slickrock Bike Trail is traversed almost
exclusively by bikes of the non-motorized variety. To cyclists, the word
"slickrock"—a generic term for sandstone outcrops found throughout
the Southwest—is a misnomer, for it's the exact opposite. The term was
coined by early settlers whose hard-metal-shod horses had trouble making the grades. But for rubber tires, slickrock—wet or dry—is like sand-
paper, and provides a remarkable degree of traction. On it, you can

ride up and down pitches impossible to negotiate on more mundane surfaces.

Make the pilgrimage to Moab and drive 3 miles east of town on paved Mill Creek Drive and Sand Flats Road. Soon after passing the most scenic town dump in the United States, you'll arrive at the parking area for the Slickrock Bike Trail (the western terminus of Kokopelli's Trail is also located here). Follow the trail's dashed white line, taking special care when approaching yellow warning paint, and attempt to stay atop your bike and free of injury. As you should everywhere in canyon country, avoid riding through the "gardens" of crusty-looking cryptogamic soil, which support growths of juniper, grasses, cacti, and other flora.

The Slickrock Bike Trail is not for the faint of heart, the weak of knee, or the short on stopping power. Be *certain* that you and your brakes are finely tuned. To understand what you're getting into, first try out the 2.3-mile "practice loop." Then you'll appreciate why it takes most riders between 4 and 6 hours to complete the 10.3-mile trail. (Most end up walking as much as riding.) In regard to the easy/moderate/hard difficulty ratings used in this guide, the Slickrock Bike Trail is way off the scale. "Extreme" best describes its difficulty.

Although the high sandstone mesa traversed by the Slickrock Bike Trail, and the views afforded from it, are spectacular, the technical challenge and the "scene" are the Trail's main draws. There are many other rides close to town that are more forgiving and whose primary attractions are the *scenery*. The three outings that follow are among Moab's most popular, so don't choose them if you're seeking solitude. But remember, there's plenty of solitude elsewhere in Utah. Enjoy Moab-area rides for what they are: well-known, highly publicized routes on which you'll have an opportunity to celebrate mountain biking's spirit of community in beautiful settings.

The supplemental maps needed for the Moab vicinity are the Moab and the La Sal 1:100,000 metric maps, available through the Bureau of Land Management, Grand Resource Area, Sand Flats Road, Moab, UT 84532, (801) 259-8193.

36. Willow Flats

Riding surface: Graded gravel, jeep trail with some sand
                       and slickrock
Elevation range: 4,620 to 5,015 feet
Distance: 8.2 miles
Relative difficulty: Easy
Time to allow: 1 to 2 hours
Best time of year: October through May
Supplemental maps: Moab 1:100,000 metric map; Arches
                       National Park visitors map

This short and easy outing will help you get your desert legs. You'll find a few hills and some great scenery, along with sprinklings of drift and wash sand, nemeses of the desert mountain biker. A side benefit reaped is the trip through scenic Arches National Park, necessary to get to the ride's beginning point.

The more than 200 catalogued arches within Arches National Park are the indirect result of salt beds, up to 2 miles thick in places, that were deposited at the bottom of a sea here millions of years ago. During the millennia that followed the sea's evaporation, sand was blown and washed in over the salt. The weight of the sand, much of it compressed into rock, was too much for the unstable salt beds, and caused them to buckle, twist, and flow. In turn, the surface rock folded, turned on edge, and collapsed into troughs in the underlying salt beds.

Water, freezing and thawing, caused shallow cracks in the surface rock to deepen; eventually long, parallel "fins" of salmon-colored Entrada Sandstone were left standing, isolated. Erosion continued, finally cutting through and creating holes in some of the fins. And the work goes on: what you see in the park today is a moment frozen in time. You can identify the remnants of previous arches, as well as structures that could well become arches in the future.

From Moab, go 4 miles north on U.S. Highway 191 and turn right into Arches National Park. Climb steadily above the river valley; 9 miles after entering the park, turn left and park at the picnic area opposite Balanced Rock.

Ride west on the high-grade gravel road, topping out at 0.2 mile with a rock quarry on the left. At 0.5 dip through a draw decorated with gnarled junipers. At 0.7 pass through a gate, after which the road deteriorates; continue straight where a fork goes right. (Eye of the Whale Arch is found about 2 miles up this fork, infamous for its sandy stretches.)

A big sky surrounds Arches National Park.

Hit a low point at 2.0 miles, then climb through a stretch of drift sand bordered on the left by a jumble of red sandstone boulders. Top out at 2.2, rolling through a semiactive dune field. Cross a sandy wash at 2.8 and follow it downstream to 3.3. Cross through the draw at 3.6 and note, down the wash to the left, the old Willow Spring cabin. Cross the draw at 3.9 on a slickrock surface and arrive at the NPS/BLM boundary, the turnaround point, at 4.1 miles.

(Note: you can continue down the road, across BLM lands, to ride a loop. You'll arrive at an extremely wide and sandy crossing of Courthouse Wash at 6.5 miles. After fighting through the sand, it's about 2 miles to U.S. Highway 191, where you turn south. In approximately 8 miles, 4 of which can be ridden on the old, decomposing highway paralleling the new road to the east, you'll arrive at the turnoff to Arches National Park. In 9 miles more, many of them along steep and narrow roadway, you'll return to the beginning point, for a total distance of about 26 miles.)

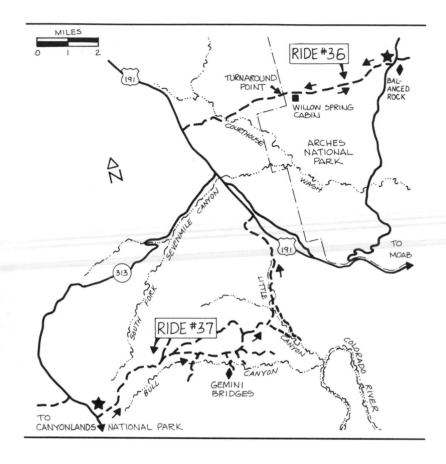

37. Gemini Bridges

Riding surface:	Smooth gravel, jeep trail
Elevation range:	4,585 to 6,010 feet
Distance:	13.9 miles
Relative difficulty:	Moderate
Time to allow:	3 to 5 hours
Best time of year:	February through May; October to November
Supplemental map:	Moab and La Sal 1:100,000 metric maps

The twins known as Gemini Bridges are two side-by-side natural bridges. Although sometimes they resemble arches, natural bridges are formed by a different process—the erosional action of stream water hitting against rock faces.

The basic point-to-point route loses 1,400 feet as it swoops down the ridge separating the Bull and South Fork Sevenmile canyons. The ride is best done with a shuttle so that every ounce of spare energy can be devoted to exploring the many intriguing spur routes branching off the main one. Even if you don't have a second vehicle at hand, the parking area mentioned below often teems with mountain bikers setting out on a similar journey, so a lift either at ride's end or beginning can probably be arranged.

If you prefer to ride a complete loop, simply pedal, rather than drive, the access route outlined below. You'll cover about 14 miles of pavement, most of them uphill, but the scenery is terrific.

From Moab, go 9.5 miles north on U.S. Highway 191 and turn left; cross the cattle guard and leave a vehicle in the wide parking area east of the railroad tracks. Continue north on U.S. Highway 191 for 1.3 miles, then turn left onto State Highway 313 toward Dead Horse Point State Park/Canyonlands National Park. After 13 miles on State Highway 313—0.8 mile past the right-hand turn to Mineral Canyon—turn left toward Gemini Bridges and park beside the highway.

Pedal downhill to the east on the main gravel road. From atop this high piñon-and-juniper-studded plateau are good views of the Henry Mountains to the west and the La Sals to the east, two of the several "intrusive igneous" ranges that rise above the otherwise sedimentary bedrock of southeast Utah.

Along the route's initial stretches, primitive paths fork left or right here and there; stick to the primary road. At 1.8 the downhill becomes a bit bouncier and at 2.2 you jostle over a cattle guard. At 3.8 continue straight as another road forks left.

At the Y at 4.0 miles bear right off the main road, toward Gemini Bridges. (The road going left rejoins the narrative below at 7.7 miles.) At 4.7 turn left at the T toward Gemini Bridges and spin through some sandy stretches (a right at this point leads to Four Arch Canyon, 2 miles away). At 5.6 the main trail continues straight/left; take the right-hand spur. It branches out into several cross-country paths, all of which lead to the Gemini Bridges. Gaze about and hike around for a while, then return to the point of departure at 6.3 miles.

Continuing along the main route, go straight at 6.5 where a right-hand spur heads to another Gemini Bridges viewpoint. After a short, rocky stretch, rather than continuing straight on what appears to be the main route, at 6.8 take the left fork and wind downhill over an expanse of slickrock. (Note: by heading straight here, you can eventually rejoin the main route at 9.1 miles. However, the trail is sometimes tough to follow; a topo map is a necessity.)

At 7.7 miles bear straight/right onto the main road coming in

from behind on your left. Head straight for the distant La Sal peaks and
the distinctive sandstone fins—or FAAs (Future Arches of America)—
situated around Behind the Rocks, largely a BLM wilderness study
area. At 8.4 the road becomes temporarily smoother; at the fork at 8.7
aim left at the rock gap in the valley below, and begin a steep downhill.

At 9.1 miles, at the base of the descent, turn left at the T and begin climbing gradually up the Little Canyon drainage, a valley filled
with sandstone caricatures. After a stretch of wash sand, continue
straight as paths veer right into side canyons at 9.3 and at 9.9. Pass
through the big gap in the cliffs at 10.4 miles.

At 11.3 the uphill intensifies as the road climbs a section of cliffs
in order to skirt the radically dissected lower, "hanging" portion of
Little Canyon. After a cattle guard, the road levels off at 11.7. Splendid
views are gained from this cliffside shelf: with binoculars, you can make
out at least one of the window arches to the northeast, in Arches National Park.

Start down at 11.9 miles. At 12.5, note distant Balanced Rock—
the beginning point for ride 36—standing between two larger, squared-
off sandstone monoliths. At 13.0 curve left onto the raised road bank
nestled between two power lines. At 13.8 curve right to cross the railroad tracks and arrive at the ride's end at 13.9 miles.

38. Hurrah Pass

Riding surface:	Pavement, smooth gravel, jeep trail
Elevation range:	4,025 to 4,740 feet
Distance:	29 miles
Relative difficulty:	Moderate
Time to allow:	4 to 7 hours
Best time of year:	February through May; October to November
Supplemental map:	Moab and La Sal 1:100,000 metric maps

Hurrah Pass commands a vista that is among the finest in Utah:
Dead Horse Point and Island in the Sky rise to the west; the slickrock
mesa that rings Moab lies to the north; to the east, the high La Sals
tower above the rim of Kane Creek Canyon. Most of the ride takes
place along well-graded paved and graveled roads that pass beneath the
sheer walls of the Colorado River and Kane Creek canyons.

A precariously perched rock near Hurrah Pass

The final 2 miles lead over a tortuous terrain of eroded Moenkopi Formation sediments. As you approach from below and look up at the gap in the rocks that is Hurrah Pass, you'll think it impossible that a road could actually lead up the cliffs. But it does. (The engineer responsible for this feat should have been awarded a medal.) Unlike some area rides, this one is good rain or shine, wet or dry. Keep a sharp eye out for carved petroglyphs as you skirt the rock walls between 3.0 and 6.0 miles.

Begin at the south end of downtown Moab, at the corner of U.S. Highway 191 and Kane Creek Boulevard. Spin northwest on Kane Creek Boulevard, at 0.7 mile bearing left off the curving road and onto Kane Creek Road (the road curving right becomes 500 West). At 1.6, at the mouth of Pack Creek, come to and begin paralleling the Colorado River along Kings Bottom. At 2.5 cross a cattle guard; spot the sandstone arch across the river and high atop the cliffs. At 3.5 pass by some habitations and mining activities.

Cross a cattle guard at 4.6; the pavement ends as the road enters Kane Springs Canyon, leaving the Colorado to its journey south. (Note: the Pritchett Canyon Trail, another popular ride, meets the road on the left just prior to the cattle guard.) At 5.4 pass a primitive road dropping right into a makeshift camping area; the uphill grade steepens beyond this point. Top out with great views at 6.2 miles, zoom down a pair of switchbacks, and regain the creek level at 6.8. On the left is a dripping spring where you'll note that beavers have felled several cottonwoods. Hoping to beaverproof the remaining trees and foil further timber harvests, someone has wrapped their trunks in sheet metal.

At 7.7 miles cross the Hunters Creek drainage. At 7.9, curve sharply left and enter an immense natural amphitheater. Top out at 10.3, enter a big, open basin, and cross through Kane Creek at 11.0 miles. Here, cottonwoods line the creek, offering good, shaded campsites. At 11.4 continue straight on the main road and leave the Kane Creek drainage (a jeep trail forks left here, following Kane Creek.) The route curves right, taking aim at Hurrah Pass.

After crossing through a draw at 11.9, the road becomes rockier, more twisting, and generally more interesting. At 12.9 begin snaking, sometimes quite steeply, up the sedimentary cliffs, passing numerous little private hideaways perfect for camping. Pass through an old fenceline at 14.3 and—Hurrah!—arrive at the pass at 14.5 miles. Spend time enjoying the views, then return to Moab the way you came.

(Note: the ride can be extended beyond Hurrah Pass. It's about 11 miles to where the road ends at a spectacular Colorado River viewpoint, via an exciting stretch of cliffside trail known as Chicken

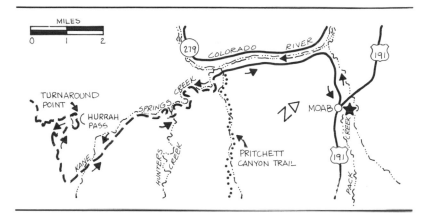

Corners—so-called because some clients of jeep-tour companies choose to walk rather than ride it. This route also ties in with a popular multi-day outing that leads through Lockhart Basin and to the Needles District of Canyonlands National Park.)

Canyon Country

In southeast Utah the Colorado and Green rivers and their myriad tributaries, large and small, have carved a huge hunk of the Colorado Plateau into a multileveled, you-can-see-it-but-can't-get-there-from-here landscape. For this reason, all five of the following are out-and-back rides rather than loops. The outings provide dramatic vistas at their turnaround points, and make ideal overnighters.

The Colorado River and Green River canyons are formidable obstacles, bridged in very few places. Glance at a map and you'll think that the rides are in close proximity to one another. Further inspection will reveal that more than 200 miles of macadam must be negotiated to get from the access point for the east-side rides to the staging areas for west-side outings.

Rides 39 and 40 are in the Needles District of Canyonlands National Park; 41 and 42 take place within Glen Canyon National Recreation Area, and provide views into the Maze District of Canyonlands. Ride 43 traverses BLM lands. None of the rides descends into the depths of the canyons. Rather, each leads to a teasing overlook. To enter the canyons is to mount an expedition; in general, mountain-bike tours into the deeper levels should be supported by vehicle. Little or no drinking water, long distances void of other people, and high temperatures make careful planning necessary. For some suggestions, see "Other Rides in Utah."

For rides 39 and 40, plan on camping at Squaw Flat Campground, 3 miles west of the Needles District visitor center. In Glen Canyon National Recreation Area and on lands administered by the BLM, venues for the other rides, free-form camping is permitted. Just remember that you can't drive or ride off the designated roadways in Glen Canyon NRA, and before spending the night you must first acquire a backcountry camping permit at the Hans Flat ranger station. Whenever staying at an undeveloped site, always depart without leaving a trace, and avoid camping within 100 feet of springs, so that the scarce water supplies remain accessible to wildlife.

The supplemental map needed for the Needles District rides is the La Sal 1:100,000 metric map, available through the Bureau of Land Management, Grand Resource Area, Sand Flats Road, Moab, UT 84532, (801) 259-8193. For the west-side rides, obtain the Hanksville 1:100,000 metric map through the Bureau of Land Management, Henry Mountain Resource Area, P.O. Box 99, Hanksville, UT, (801) 542-3461. You'll also find useful the Canyonlands National Park and Glen Canyon NRA visitors maps.

39. Colorado River Overlook

Riding surface:	Jeep trail with some sandy and slickrock sections
Elevation range:	4,760 to 4,920 feet
Distance:	15 miles
Relative difficulty:	Moderate
Time to allow:	2 to 4 hours
Best time of year:	February through May; October to November
Supplemental maps:	La Sal 1:100,000 metric map; Canyonlands National Park visitors map

From this ride's turnaround point, which overlooks the lower Salt Creek and Colorado River canyons, you can see forever. To the left are the namesake Needles of Canyonlands; Junction Butte stands directly in front, and to its right are Island in the Sky and Dead Horse Point. Below the top of the Island you can see the White Rim. The La Sal Mountains rise from behind the cliffs of the Canyon Rims Recreation Area; opposite are the Abajo, or Blue, Mountains. Desert bighorns sometimes can be seen along the route.

From 14 miles north of Monticello, or 40 miles south of Moab, on U.S. Highway 191, go west on State Highway 211 for 36 miles to the modular national park visitor center. En route, stop and study Newspaper Rock, one of the most pictograph-decorated rock faces in Utah.

From the visitor center, head north on the gravel road signed "Colorado Overlook 7." At 0.1 mile pass through a fenceline and fork left, coasting downhill. Hit a short stretch of sand at 0.7 mile.

Skirt the bottom of Salt Creek at 1.0 as you roll amidst the animated shapes of Cedar Mesa Sandstone. In the 1.6 vicinity, note Junction Butte directly in front and Island in the Sky to its right.

Cross a small wash at 2.2 and at 2.7 arrive at Salt Creek. Hike (riding off the road is illegal) down the trail to the left for 0.25 mile to see the lower "jump"—or abrupt drop-off—of Salt Creek. Water cascading over the rimrock creates a picturesque falls.

At 2.8 begin gradually up; to your left in the distance notice the Needles, a jumble of spires and monoliths formed by erosion of the

Prehistoric headlines decorate Newspaper Rock

Cedar Mesa Sandstone. At 3.3 encounter a long stretch of slickrock, and begin coasting down at 3.8. Cross a small wash at 4.2, then climb from 4.4 to 4.7 miles. Between the canyon bottom and the top of Island in the Sky, note the horizontal layer of white sandstone. The

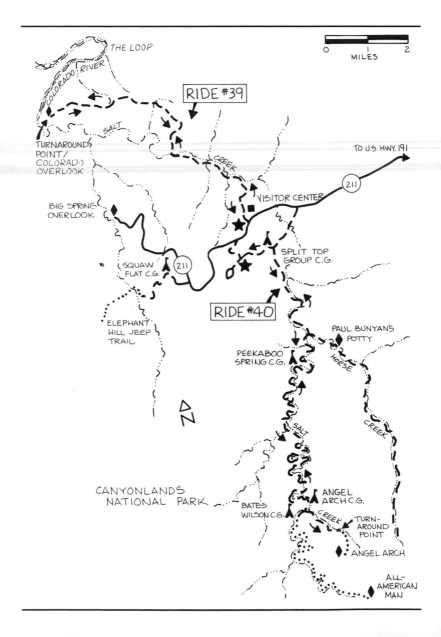

White Rim Trail, a very popular multiday jeep/mountain-bike trail, traverses this rim of the Island (see "Other Rides in Utah").

At 5.0, brushing against a canyon rim on your right, you can see The Loop, a gooseneck formed where the Colorado River doubles back on itself. Beginning at 6.0 is a mile-plus stretch of slickrock that dishes up a riding challenge and a load of fun. At 7.3 begin down and at 7.5 arrive at the parking area. You must walk a couple of hundred feet to get to the breathtaking, knee-weakening overlooks. On the left is the deep canyon of Salt Creek, nearing its confluence with the Colorado, whose canyon spreads out for miles, right and left. Everywhere lies a vastly different scene; take a good, long look.

40. Anasazi Wonderland

Riding surface:	Jeep trail with deep wash sand and rocky stream bottom
Elevation range:	4,930 to 5,480 feet
Distance:	27 miles
Relative difficulty:	Hard
Time to allow:	6 to 10 hours
Best time of year:	February through April
Supplemental maps:	La Sal 1:100,000 metric map; Canyonlands National Park visitors map

This ride penetrates the Salt Creek Archaeological District, placed on the National Register of Historic Places in 1977. The canyon provides good soil, a reliable water source, and abundant game, all rarities in these parts. Combined, they account for the extraordinary concentration of Anasazi granaries—evidence of intensive agricultural activity—and other ruins found in the wildly meandering Salt Creek Canyon. The Mesa Verde Anasazis lived in Salt Creek Canyon and adjacent canyons from approximately 1050 A.D. to 1200 A.D., and Indians of the Archaic culture preceded them here by at least 7,000 years.

Fremont-style rock art is found on panels throughout the canyons, but, strangely, there is no other evidence linking the Fremonts to the vicinity. The Fremont Indians occupied central Utah when the Anasazis lived here; perhaps the Anasazi copied the Fremont-style art they had seen elsewhere in Utah.

The rewards gained in accomplishing this ride are tremendous. In addition to the Indian ruins and rock art, you will see beautifully graceful Angel Arch, the Kissing Camels formation, and numerous side canyons ideal for exploring by foot. Fittingly, you must put in at least one day's hard work to reap the benefits. Depending on the time of year and recent weather conditions, there can be between 1 and 2 miles of walk-ing-necessary, deep, dry-wash sand to negotiate en route to Peekaboo Spring. The cycling conditions improve beyond there.

Up to a point, the best time to ride here is after a rainfall or snow-melt, for moisture compacts the loose sand. Too much precipitation, however, and sections of quicksand can appear, which is no fun at all to deal with. Check with NPS personnel at the visitor center for current conditions.

If you have a four-wheel-drive vehicle, or can arrange for a lift in someone else's to the Peekaboo Spring Campground, so much the bet-ter. But if you can't, simply walk the sandy stretches and think like a hiker (pushing a bicycle) rather than a mountain biker. To see what you'll see and ride what you'll ride beyond Peekaboo Spring, this—along with some grit in your bike's moving parts—is a reasonable price to pay.

To do them justice, two or three days should be devoted to ex-ploring these canyons. For example, on day one ride to Angel Arch, then back to Angel Arch Campground or down to Bates Wilson Camp-ground (named after the legendary man who instigated creation of the national park and for eight years served as its first superintendent). On the next day, pedal the short distance to the Upper Salt Creek Trail-head. From there it's an 11-mile round-trip hike to All American Man, a red-white-and-blue pictograph that must be seen to be believed. It's about 15 miles round trip if you continue down to Wedding Ring Arch and the nearby Big Ruin, Canyonlands' most extensive ruins, with 32 dwelling and storage structures.

Finally, when cycling and walking back to your car, consider turn-ing off to explore Horse Canyon, another Anasazi hotbed and home to a curious sandstone feature known as Paul Bunyan's Potty.

From the Needles District visitor center (see access directions for ride 39), go west. In approximately 0.5 mile, turn south toward Salt Creek and park at the T in 0.7 mile.

Turn left, riding along the graded gravel road (right goes toward the ranger residences). At 0.8 mile, just past the Split Top Group Campsite, turn right toward Salt Creek, where going straight leads to Cave Spring. Cross through the sandy wash bottom at 0.9, and at 1.2 come to a set of signs describing the archaeological district and warning of the four-wheel-drive-necessary conditions of the road ahead.

From 1.4 to 3.6 go upstream along the bottom of the Salt Creek drainage. Some stretches may be ridable; at worst, you'll have a soft-footed, 2-mile hike. Slow down, since you have no choice, and enjoy. Look and listen for the abundant bird life along the riparian corridor.

Graceful Angel Arch, one of Canyonlands' most beautiful, yet least-visited, sights

Bluebirds, especially, stand out brightly against the earth tones of the landscape.

At the fork at 3.6, bear right toward Salt Creek; the left-hand fork leads up Horse Canyon. At 4.7 you come to Peekaboo Spring, with its campground, unique Anasazi-on-Archaic pictographs, and peekaboo hole in the rock. The trail loops back on itself, presenting at 5.1 a look at the other side of the hole.

Roll by an immense, natural amphitheater on the right at 5.6, then zip through the creek three times in 100 yards. As you proceed up the canyon, watch for waterfowl floating on backwaters and for mule deer. In and out of the water, at times the trail has no choice but to follow the creek bottom itself, as it does for an 80-yard stretch at 7.5 miles. Sections of the trail are very rocky and strewn with river cobbles.

At a lone, gnarled cottonwood tree on the right, immediately prior to a creek crossing at 8.1, look up at the cliffs to the right. Here you'll see one of the canyon's many Anasazi granaries. It's easy to spot if the cliffs are in the shade, but tough if the sun is hitting them.

At 9.4 miles top out on a rise between two creek crossings, and resume rock-'n'-rolling through the streambed at 9.9. You're up the creek between 10.6 and 11.0. At 12.0 pass Angel Arch Campground on the left; at 12.2 turn left toward Angel Arch and cross through the stream. (Turn right for the 0.5-mile approach to the hiking trail that continues up Salt Creek Canyon to All-American Man and other previously mentioned attractions.)

Leaving the water, climb steeply for 100 yards and continue gradually uphill across the sand and rocks. At 12.5, up on the cliffs to the left, is a large, symmetrical granary. At 13.5 arrive at the turnaround point and the trailhead for the short hike to Angel Arch.

41. Panorama Point

Riding surface:	Jeep trail with some sand and rock
Elevation range:	6,160 to 6,650 feet
Distance:	17 miles
Relative difficulty:	Moderate
Time to allow:	3 to 5 hours
Best time of year:	March through May; September through November
Supplemental maps:	Hanksville 1:100,000 metric map; Canyonlands National Park visitors map

The name says it all. From Panorama Point you see, from an altogether different perspective, many of the same features seen from the Colorado River Overlook (ride 39). Spread out before you is a visual feast that includes the following: Island in the Sky, the La Sal Mountains, the very tip-top peaks of the distant San Juan Range in Colorado, the Needles, the Maze, the Abajos, the Land of Standing Rocks, and much more.

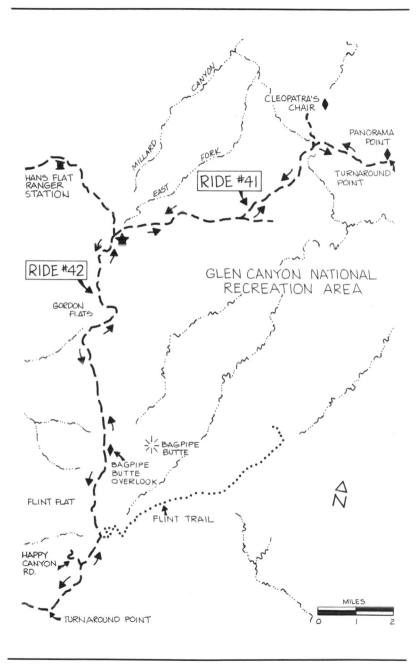

CANYON

CLEOPATRA'S
CHAIR

PANORAMA
POINT

MILLARD

FORK

TURNAROUND
POINT

HANS FLAT
RANGER
STATION

EAST

RIDE #41

RIDE #42

GLEN CANYON NATIONAL
RECREATION AREA

GORDON
FLATS

BAGPIPE
BUTTE

BAGPIPE
BUTTE
OVERLOOK

N

FLINT FLAT

FLINT TRAIL

HAPPY
CANYON
RD.

TURNAROUND POINT

MILES

0   1   2

Looking out at the goal, Panorama Point

The ride follows a rolling, timbered rim high above the canyon bottom. Camping at the turnaround point is permitted and recommended. Just remember: you're not allowed to ride off the designated jeep trail, and you must pick up a backcountry camping permit at the Hans Flat ranger station, which serves as the area headquarters for both Canyonlands National Park and Glen Canyon NRA.

You lose elevation en route to Panorama Point, so the ride back is tougher and includes some walking-permitted hills. You'll see terrific views of the Henry Mountains that you may not have noticed on the northbound approach to Panorama Point.

Twenty-three miles south of Interstate 70, or 14 miles north of Hanksville, on State Highway 24—between mileposts 136 and 137—turn east onto gravel toward "Hans Flat/Park Ranger" and drive the 45 long and deserted miles to the Hans Flat ranger station. (This access road itself can be a fun ride, except for occasional stretches of deep sand and bumpy washboard.) From the ranger station, continue south toward the Flint Trail for 2.5 miles and park your car at the turn to Panorama Point.

Follow the four-wheel-drive road northeast, alternating between stretches of up and down, and encountering occasional sandy sections. Top out at 1.5 and at 2.1 coast down into a broad, relatively verdant flat. It's mostly down to 2.8; from there, climb for 0.5 mile to reach another flat area.

Continue straight down the steep hill at 3.9 miles (the right-hand fork accesses a terrific canyon overlook and hiking trail in 0.5 mile.) Bottom out at 4.8 and climb to 5.2; from here you can see Panorama Point jutting out to the right. At the bottom of a radical descent, you skirt the precipitous canyon rim at 5.7.

At 6.8 turn right toward Panorama Point (a left turn leads 2 miles to Cleopatra's Chair). Climb to 7.0, go down a short hill, and continue gradually up along some technical stretches of slickrock and sand. At 8.5 miles is Panorama Point, an ideal setting for a campsite; it's studded with piñons and junipers, punctuated with smaller yucca and Mormon tea plants. This is the turnaround point, and one of the best vistas in canyon country.

42. Lands End: The Sequel

Riding surface:	Jeep trail with some sand and rock
Elevation range:	6,390 to 6,990 feet
Distance:	25.2 miles
Relative difficulty:	Moderate
Time to allow:	4 to 6 hours
Best time of year:	March through May; September through November
Supplemental maps:	Hanksville 1:100,000 metric map; Canyonlands National Park visitors map

Although the names are identical and fewer than 200 miles separate the two, this Lands End is a world apart from Colorado's Lands End, featured in ride 15. The first 3 miles of the trip can be quite sandy, if you prefer to bypass them, simply drive ahead and start riding wherever suits your fancy. The solitude this ride provides makes it easy to believe that the Maze District of Canyonlands is among the most remote and least-visited areas of any national park in the Lower 48.

The route traverses high, timbered plateau country similar to that encountered on ride 41. Several primitive campsites beckon near the ride's awesome ending point, where you'll look out over Waterhole Flat and the deep canyon of the Colorado River to the south and, to the north, the shallower but impressive forks of Happy Canyon, which wind down to join the Dirty Devil River canyon. Because you're within

Glen Canyon NRA, you can camp anywhere, as long as you acquire a free backcountry camping permit and don't take your bike off the road.

At the turnoff to Panorama Point (see access directions for ride 41), continue biking south along the main route toward the Flint Trail. The first 3 miles are alternately up and down, through sometimes-deep sand. After rolling across a wide flat, at 3.3 miles you begin coasting through an area decorated with big sandstone outcrops. Beginning at 3.8 climb toward Gordon Flats, topping out at 4.5 miles.

At 5.1 is a 0.5-mile stretch of potentially troublesome sand; at 5.6 on the left you pass an enclosure that demonstrates how vegetated the countryside here could be in the absence of "slow elk" (also known as domestic cattle). At 6.4 the Bagpipe Butte Overlook is on the left; cross over a cattle guard.

Continuing up and down, pass through Flint Flat at 8.8 miles. At 9.6 bear right toward Big Ridge/Lands End as the Flint Trail goes left to begin its canyon plunge. Spin gradually uphill amidst the piñons and junipers as the road becomes decidedly a jeep trail.

At 10.5 miles continue straight along the narrowing Lands End as Happy Canyon Road, an interesting spur route, goes right. The road turns rough, rocky, and downright gnarly for the next couple of miles. At 11.8 you arrive at the pinched-neck land bridge that provides long-range views right and left. Continue over slickrock and broken rock to 12.6, the recommended turnaround point, where you'll find many good camping spots. (The jeep trail continues westward along Big Ridge for a few miles, becoming extremely rugged and eventually very sandy.)

43. Dance with the Dirty Devil

Riding surface: Smooth gravel with some sand
Elevation range: 4,890 to 5,530 feet
Distance: 21.2 miles
Relative difficulty: Easy
Time to allow: 3 to 5 hours
Best time of year: October through April
Supplemental maps: Hanksville 1:100,000 metric map, Glen
                     Canyon NRA visitors map

Winding up and down through the rolling Burr Desert, this ride's goal is impressive Burr Point. From here you can look out across the canyon of the Dirty Devil River, allegedly named when the intrepid

John Wesley Powell was asked if the waters were good for trout fishing. "No, it's a dirty devil," Powell replied.

Large cattle ranches popped up in the area in the early 1900s, but rustlers and recurrent drought made it a tough go. Twelve miles north of Burr Point, Robbers Roost Canyon feeds into the Dirty Devil River from the east. Lying along the Outlaw Trail, which ranged from Canada to Mexico, the canyon was a popular hideout for notorious notables such as Butch Cassidy and Harry Longbaugh, a.k.a. the Sundance Kid. After experiencing a ride in this country, you'll appreciate how easy it must have been for rustlers and other undesirables to keep themselves unfound in the abundant hard-to-access sidecanyons of the river.

From the desert outpost of Hanksville, go 16 miles south on State Highway 95 and park near the left-hand turn signed "Dirty Devil River Overlook 11." Passenger-car friendly, this road's traffic can pick up on weekends; weekdays are your best bet.

Start gradually uphill through blackbrush flats along the delightfully curving and roller-coaster-like road. The views are broad and long-

The Dirty Devil route meanders across the Burr Desert; the Henry Mountains rise in the background.

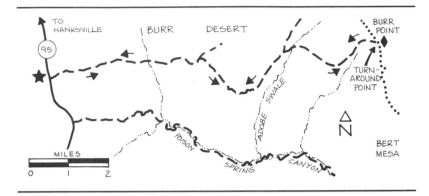

ranging in this open, shadeless country. Top out temporarily at 1.2 and head down toward the buff-red canyon ahead. You bottom out in a sandy section at 1.8, where a primitive road forks left; continue up along the main road.

At 2.0 top out on a rise with expansive, 360-degree views. Behind, the laccolithic Henry Mountains erupt splendidly from the desert floor. At 3.0 bottom out where a primitive road forks right; continue up. Curve right out of a drainage bottom at 3.5 miles, as a rough road forks right toward some corrals.

At 4.4, as the route curves right, a primitive road forks left toward some intriguing sandstone outcrops. Dip and rise through a series of *yee-haw* draw crossings during the next 0.5 mile. At 4.9 crest a ridge and go down.

Resume uphill riding at 5.1 miles, occasionally dipping down through a drainage. At 7.8 continue straight where a road forks left and skirt to the left of the slickrock expanses of Adobe Swale, which leads south into Poison Spring Canyon. At 10.6 you reach the turnaround point and the overlook into the Dirty Devil River canyon. Directly ahead is Sams Mesa Box Canyon; to the right is the mouth of Happy Canyon, the drainage whose source is skirted on ride 42.

(Note: you might be able to complete a loop by following the jeep trail leading south from Burr Point, crossing over Bert Mesa, and heading into the Dirty Devil River canyon. You would ultimately head downstream through Poison Spring Canyon and hit State Highway 95 at a point 1.5 miles south of the Dirty Devil Overlook turnoff. For current trail conditions, inquire at the BLM's Henry Mountain Resource Area office in Hanksville.)

Bluff–Mexican Hat

Mexican Hat, Bluff, and the other towns and visitors' attractions in the extreme southeastern corner of Utah are linked by what the state and San Juan County travel bureaus have dubbed "the Trail of the Ancients." And ancient the trail is—for instance, a Paleo Indian site, at least 10,000 years old, was discovered recently atop Lime Ridge, which lies near U.S. Highway 163, midway between rides 44 and 45. Good rides are located all along the trail, so it's well worth driving (see "Other Rides in Utah").

The Anasazi settled heavily in this area; it appears that late in the thirteenth century they abandoned all of southeast Utah and southwest Colorado and moved to the south. Dozens of Anasazi ruins can be seen along the Trail of the Ancients; probably the most impressive collection is the one at Hovenweep National Monument, along the Utah-Colorado border.

This land is still active Indian country today. The 16-million-acre Navajo Reservation extends from Arizona north into Utah, to the banks of the San Juan River. The *Diné,* relative newcomers to the Southwest, migrated into the region not long after the Anasazi dispersed.

Bluff, the first white community in southeast Utah, was settled during the winter of 1879-80, when a large group of Mormons traveled south to here from the town of Escalante, via the Hole in the Rock Trail. Several of their original sandstone-block houses still stand, testimonies to Bluff's past. Comb Ridge, the focus of ride 45, helped to direct the Mormons' route; from the Abajo Mountains south to Kayenta, Arizona, the abrupt monocline was essentially uncrossable—especially by a party that included 83 horse-drawn wagons and 1,000 head of cattle—except at the point south of San Juan Hill where the San Juan River cuts through it.

Consider basing out of the no-water-available campground at Goosenecks State Park, 8 miles north and west of Mexican Hat. Here, the San Juan River has cut entrenched meanders nearly 2,000 feet deep in the Colorado Plateau. From the campground, you can look down on the goosenecks and across the river to the Navajo Nation's Monument Valley.

The supplemental maps needed for the Bluff-Mexican Hat vicinity are the Bluff and the Blanding 1:100,000 metric maps, available through the Bureau of Land Management, San Juan Resource Area, 435 North Main, Monticello, UT 84535, (801) 587-2141.

One of many sandstone idols in the Valley of the Gods

44. Valley of the Gods Loop

Riding surface:	Pavement and graded dirt road with some rocky stretches
Elevation range:	4,400 to 5,305 feet
Distance:	26.7 miles
Relative difficulty:	Moderate
Time to allow:	4 to 6 hours
Best time of year:	February through May; October to November
Supplemental maps:	Bluff 1:100,000 metric map

This route winds through Valley of the Gods, which is like a small-scale version of nearby Monument Valley (the latter can be seen to the south during your ride). As you brush against Cedar Mesa, it's easy to envision how at one time the isolated pillars and monoliths rising from the desert were part of the mesa. In good weather the dirt road leading through Valley of the Gods is negotiable by passenger cars, yet very few of them find the way to this remote corner of the Beehive State.

If by chance you're carrying a portable radio, tune in to Window Rock, AM 660 on your dial. You could find yourself riding to the sounds of Navajo chanting, which is like conjuring the gods of this isolated valley and hearing them, magically, speak.

From Goosenecks State Park, head northeast on State Highway 316; in just over 3 miles, park at the junction with State Highway 261. (This point is about 4 miles north and west of the river-rat settlement of Mexican Hat.) Ride west on State Highway 261, which here is narrow and lacks a good shoulder. The sight distances are long and the traffic typically low, however.

After a short downhill at 1.1, the road levels off again. As you aim straight for Cedar Mesa, you might ask yourself how the main highway could possibly climb its apparently vertical cliffs. It is an engineering wonder for 3 miles the paved road turns to gravel as it switchbacks up the white-knuckle-forming Moki Dugway, gaining 1,100 feet by the time it reaches the mesa's top. (Note: at the top of the Moki Dugway, where the pavement resumes, a fun riding road leads south for 3.8 miles to Muley Point, an overlook where you'll see the San Juan River's goosenecks, Monument Valley, Navajo Mountain, the Henry and Abajo mountains, and more.)

At 3.0 coast downhill and cross a draw at 3.5 miles. At 5.5—

thankfully, just before the highway begins climbing the dugway—turn right toward Valley of the Gods and Lee's Dude Ranch. Pass the ranch on your left at 5.9. Signed "Camping Available," it's the only settlement for miles around. Begin a long downhill trend.

At 6.5 begin coasting beside a draw on your left; buttes, spires, towers, and all kinds of inanimate creatures surround you. At 7.0 dip through the draw and climb out. The road is becoming narrow, winding, and fascinating in nature. Coast through a small draw at 9.1, then through a major drainage at 9.3 miles. Climbing out, take aim at Balanced Rock and begin regaining the elevation lost.

Start climbing in earnest at 10.5, cresting a ridge at 10.8 miles and skirting the wildly dissected fringes of Cedar Mesa. Cross through a draw at 11.0; the road climbs as it skirts the mesa's extending fingers.

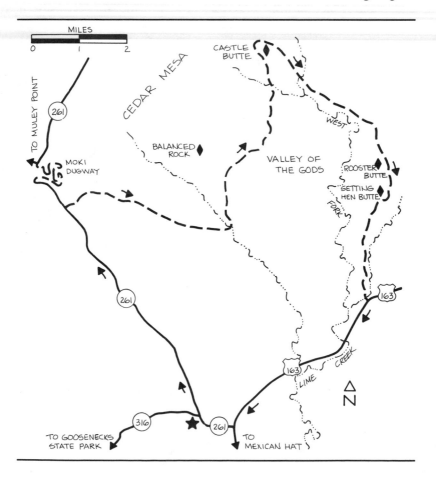

By 13.9 you're into a stand of scattered juniper. Twisting and turning, at 14.3 crest the saddle separating Castle Butte, on your right, from the long ridge coming down off Cedar Mesa. Coast into a new world.

At 15.9 zip through the West Fork Lime Creek drainage and climb for 0.5 mile. Continuing the downhill trend, by 17.3 miles the road has straightened out, but the scenery is still convoluted and grand. On the right at 18.5 are Rooster and Setting Hen buttes; at 18.9 sidehill along the eastern slope of the latter.

Rounding a right-hand curve at 19.1, you're greeted by a terrific overview of Valley of the Gods and its distant Monument Valley backdrop. At 19.8, one terrace above the Lime Creek bottoms, pass through some semistabilized sand dunes. At 21.7 miles cross Lime Creek and turn right onto wide U.S. Highway 163. At 25.8, at Mexican Hat Junction, bear right onto State Highway 261 and close the loop at 26.7 miles.

45. Comb Ridge Loop

Riding surface:	Dirt road with some sandy stretches, pavement
Elevation range:	4,380 to 5,460 feet
Distance:	47.3 miles
Relative difficulty:	Moderate
Time to allow:	10 hours to 2 days
Best time of year:	February through May; October to November
Supplemental maps:	Bluff and Blanding 1:100,000 metric maps

This route loops around a large portion of Comb Ridge, passing *through* it in the excavations of U.S. Highway 163 and State Highway 95. Best done as a 2-day outing, only particularly strong and ambitious riders (with a large water supply) should attempt to complete the loop in 1 day. Much of the route turns to muck after rain; conversely, after a very dry period the route's sandy stretches will slow you down. Choose your day accordingly.

Comb Ridge, a monocline formed by the folding of the earth's surface in only one direction, is 80 miles long and runs north-south. Initially following Comb Wash upstream, the route parallels the abrupt west side of the ridge. After tracing the highway through the northern portion of Comb Ridge, the route turns south to follow Butler Wash, skirting the ridge's gentler, user-friendly east side.

For a shorter day outing, some variation of the Butler Wash portion of the ride is recommended. Here, dozens of side canyons—some hiding Anasazi treasures—invite exploration by foot, and the Bears Ears of the Abajo Mountains, a familiar sight along the Trail of the Ancients, rise dramatically in the distance. A simple "out and back" of a few miles, beginning just west of Bluff, would make a dandy ride.

From Bluff, go 5 miles west on U.S. Highway 163 and park at the right-hand turnoff to Butler Wash Road/County Road 230.

Coast downhill to the west on U.S. Highway 163 and cross Butler Wash at 0.6. Begin climbing, at 1.6 finding yourself surrounded by the ancient sediments that lie within Comb Ridge. Coast down to cross Comb Wash at 2.2 and start up; at 2.8 miles turn right onto Comb Wash Road/County Road 235.

You begin to gain elevation as you head north; the stark red walls of Comb Ridge loom on the right. Providing a thrill a minute, the path twists and turns, dipping through and climbing out of the many side drainages flowing from the west into Comb Wash. At 5.2 miles follow the right-hand fork where a similar-surface road goes left. (Note: this is where the Mormons' Hole in the Rock Trail joins Comb Wash. A fine ride, the trail begins not far from Natural Bridges National Monument and follows primitive roads for 30 miles to this point.)

A sandstone-block house in Bluff stands as testimony to the past.

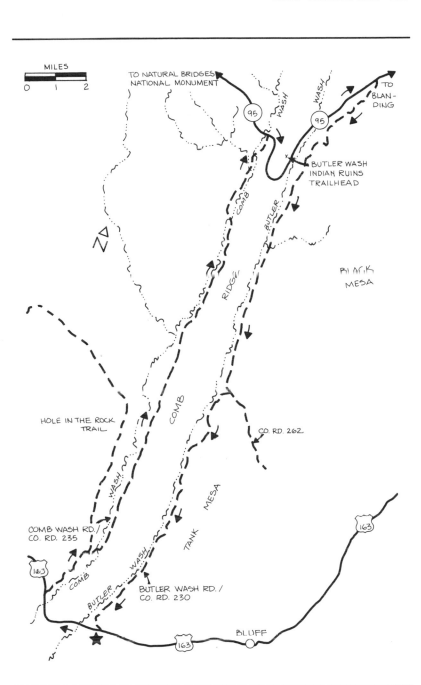

MILES

0   1   2

TO NATURAL BRIDGES
NATIONAL MONUMENT

TO
BLAN-
DING

95

95

WASH

WASH

BUTLER WASH
INDIAN RUINS
TRAILHEAD

COMB

BUTLER

RIDGE

BLACK
MESA

N

HOLE IN THE ROCK
TRAIL

COMB

WASH

CO. RD. 262

COMB WASH RD. /
CO. RD. 235

163

COMB

BUTLER

WASH

TANK   MESA

163

BUTLER WASH RD. /
CO. RD. 230

163   BLUFF

Pass through the wide Comb Wash at 5.6 miles and then a couple of other draws prior to crossing a cattle guard at 8.2. Twist and turn your way to another cattle guard crossing at 11.5. At 11.8 a primitive road forks left; continue along Comb Wash as the road levels and straightens and dishes up some additional sandy stretches.

At 14.9 enter an area of low-lying sandstone bluffs rising to the left, in the direction of the Fish Creek BLM Wilderness Study Area; here, cottonwoods grow from the banks of Comb Wash. At 16.7 coast back down to the drainage bottom and pass a road accessing a primitive campsite on the left at 16.9 miles. Pass through a gate at 17.0. The low, pale, beautifully stratified cliffs on the left contrast dramatically with the hard, sheer, red walls of Comb Ridge.

At 17.9 dip through the wash and climb back out. At 19.5 you begin to see the scarring evidence of ORVs off to the left. At 19.7 cross through the wash, spotting the highway cut ahead on the right. Again ride through the wash at 20.5, pass an outhouse on the left at 21.0, and at 21.2 turn right onto State Highway 95 to begin climbing.

Make a second pass through Comb Ridge at 22.5 miles. Emerging on the ridge's east side, where it's possible to dismount and climb to its top, coast to 23.6 and again begin up. On the left is a rest area and the trailhead to Butler Wash Indian Ruins. About 1 mile long, the trail leads to a viewpoint overlooking the 20-room Anasazi cliff house and a number of adjacent storage structures.

Climb to 26.0 and turn right onto Butler Wash Road. Curve right through a big draw at 26.3 and begin edging up the timbered rimrock, viewing the folded, eroded, and light-colored eastern side of Comb Ridge. (There are some outstanding camping spots in this vicinity.) Zipping into and climbing out of drainage after drainage, at 29.4 pass through a fenceline. At 30.0 the road straightens, but continues crossing numerous side drainages cut into the western slope of Black Mesa.

At 30.9 continue straight as a primitive track forks left. Cross through a fenceline at 34.4 and spot a deep cave on the side of Comb Ridge. Cross a cattle guard at 36.7, pass through a draw at 37.1, then arrive at a junction. Go right to continue paralleling Butler Wash and Comb Ridge, rather than left onto County Road 262.

At 37.5 bear left on the main track and pass through a fenceline at 38.9 miles. Here, a road joins in from behind on the left. At 40.0 go left on the main track. At 44.2 begin winding up onto the slopes of Tank Mesa; on the right at 45.2 Butler Wash opens into a deep cleft in the sandstone. Cross a cattle guard at 46.2 and at 46.9 go left onto the graveled road. Pass through a gate and close the loop at 47.3 miles.

Riding the slickrock, San Rafael Reef

Reef Country

Reef. Webster's defines it as "a ridge of rocks or sand at or near the surface of the water." So, where's the water and what are reefs doing out here in the middle of the desert? Did the tips of these impressive cliffs once protrude from a vast sea?

No. The term was adapted by early prospectors and other pioneers, many of them nautical men, to describe these barriers to free movement. Of the many intense folds that occurred while the Colorado Plateau was being uplifted, few resulted in cliffs as impressive as those formed by Capitol Reef, which flanks the Waterpocket Fold, and the San Rafael Reef, adjacent to the San Rafael Swell.

Thanks go to the buff-colored Navajo Sandstone's wind-deposited sediments, for wherever the erosion-resistant Navajo crops out, once the softer materials surrounding it have been washed away, it's left standing to form steep, rounded cliffs, or "hogbacks."

Similar forces created Capitol Reef and the San Rafael Reef, and their cliffs and adjacent uplifted terrain have much in common. But, whereas Capitol Reef is a widely known attraction, few people have heard of the San Rafael Reef country. Nevertheless, lately it has been getting some deserved respect: several potential BLM wilderness areas are being evaluated within the swell. Some folks even go so far as to maintain that this area, like Capitol Reef, should be a national park, but the many exploratory roads and scars from mining will likely prevent this.

Reef Country offers some of the finest exploring to be found in the region, whether on bicycle or, where two-wheelers are not practical or legal, on foot. You'll discover arches, pinnacles, and spires, and hidden canyons with steep walls covered in desert varnish, often decorated with Indian rock art. On the San Rafael Reef certain expanses of slickrock, which is virtually impervious to fat tires, are legal venues. (Conversely, as in all national parks, at Capitol Reef you must adhere to the designated roads and jeep trails.)

The supplemental maps needed for Reef Country are the San Rafael Desert, Loa, and Salina 1:100,000 metric maps, available through the Bureau of Land Management, Henry Mountain Resource Area, P.O. Box 99, Hanksville, UT 84734, (801) 542-3461.

46. Little Wild Horse Whirl

Riding surface:	Graded dirt road with some wash sand
Elevation range:	4,750 to 5,030 feet
Distance:	21.2 miles
Relative difficulty:	Easy
Time to allow:	3 to 5 hours
Best time of year:	February through May; October to November
Supplemental map:	San Rafael Desert 1:100,000 metric map

Skirting beneath the San Rafael Reef to the east, this ride tempts and invites you to hike into a couple of its classic slot canyons. The road is adjacent to the Crack Canyon Wilderness Study Area, so off-road travel by bike is taboo.

The ride begins at the developed campground in Goblin Valley State Park, home to thousands of odd little sculptures of eroded Entrada Sandstone. Standing about comically and as if in formation, the "goblins" seem prepared at any moment to march away and fight some mythical battle.

From 22 miles south of Interstate 70, or 15 miles north of

Hanksville, on State Highway 24 (between mileposts 136 and 137, approximately 0.5 mile north of the turn to Hans Flat), turn west onto a paved road leading toward Goblin Valley State Park. At 5.2 miles turn left, following the sign pointing toward the reserve. Proceed for 7 miles on gravel to the campground, en route paying at the self-service entrance station.

Pedal north from the campground, leaving the state park. At 1.0 turn left onto the smooth dirt road at the sign reading "Wild Horse Butte," which is the high mesa on the left. Heading uphill at first, soon you begin a gradual, 2-mile descent. Cross over a cattle guard at 2.4, taking care not to pass directly over its center, where there's a tire-eating gap in the grates.

At 2.6 bear right at the fork and at 3.2 miles spin across the sandy bottom of the Wild Horse Creek drainage. Start descending gradually toward the hard rock of the reef. On the left at 3.6, through the drainage notch of Wild Horse Creek, you can see the Henry Mountains standing sentinel over the desert.

At 4.9 pass through a fenceline and begin a stretch of steeper climbing, skirting the reef on your right. Hit a high point at 5.4, coast down for 0.2 mile, and resume climbing. Top out at 5.9, continuing straight as a primitive road forks left. Drop quickly to 6.4 miles, where the grade diminishes and you enter the bottom of the Little Wild Horse drainage. Consider stashing your bike here and walking upcanyon; about 0.5 mile north of the road, Bell and Little Wild Horse canyons split, both offering fascinating slot-canyon hiking (Bell goes left, Little Wild Horse right).

The downstream spin through the wash is alternately hard-packed

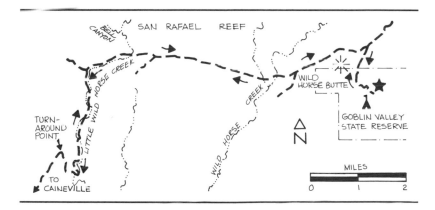

Little Wild Horse Whirl flanks the San Rafael Reef.

and sandy. At 7.6 miles curve left as a primitive road goes right up an unnamed canyon. As you pedal beneath the steep cliffs, note that their walls of uniform, horizontal strata are occasionally disrupted by dikes running at odd angles. At 10.1, after the long downcanyon cruise, begin ascending away from the draw; at 10.3 switchback right and start climbing steeply.

Top out at 10.6. Although the road continues, dropping into the valley of Muddy Creek and eventually leading to Caineville, this is the recommended turnaround point. From here you reap terrific views of the mountains and mesas to the south and west: of Capitol Reef, Thousand Lake Mountain, Boulder Top, Factory Butte, the Henrys. Note that, as the crow flies, you're only about 15 miles from a portion of the Cathedral Valley Loop (ride 48). For an even broader outlook on things, hike up onto Little Wild Horse Mesa, to the right.

47. Temple Mountain Loop

Riding surface: Pavement, rugged jeep trail, wash sand
Elevation range: 5,210 to 6,745 feet
Distance: 18.5 miles
Relative difficulty: Moderate
Time to allow: 3 to 5 hours
Best time of year: March through May; September to
                    November
Supplemental map: San Rafael Desert 1:100,000 metric map

Looping around distinctive Temple Mountain, named for its resemblance to the Mormon temple in Salt Lake City, this ride dishes up a cross section of the swell's diverse terrain—from slot canyons to high, timbered mesas—and will leave you anxious to investigate more of this country. Fortunately, there's a lot more of it: the swell extends both northeast and southwest of Interstate 70 for some 40 miles, and averages 20 miles in width. (For some suggestions, see "Other Rides in Utah.")

Although no one lives here now, evidence abounds of man's past activities around Temple Mountain. You'll spot Fremont pictographs and see relics from uranium- and radium-mining days. (A note of caution: heavy concentrations of radon gas are said to build up around the entrances to the old mines, so potential collapse is not the only danger faced when entering a shaft. To be safe, view them from a distance.)

Park 7 miles north of Goblin Valley State Park, at the junction of the gravel and paved roads (see access directions for ride 46). Ride west on the pavement, penetrating the San Rafael Reef via South Temple Wash. As you roll amidst the convoluted-cowpie, frozen-dune slickrock of Navajo Sandstone, Temple Mountain, the highest point along the reef, rises to the right. Once behind the swell's first sandstone wall of defense, piñons and junipers sprout in the protected niches where soil has accumulated.

Just shy of 1.0, veer right onto the path going into a parking area. On the cliff face above, note the Fremont shield-type pictographs carved in the desert-varnish veneer. Originally they extended farther west, but the surface rock has broken away, carrying the ancient carvings with it.

Coast through the wash at 1.1. The pavement ends at 1.3 miles; continue climbing on a high-grade gravel surface, surrounded by massive rock outcrops. Go straight where a dirt path forks right at 1.8 miles. (Note: turn right here for a shorter loop of 7.6 miles. Hugging

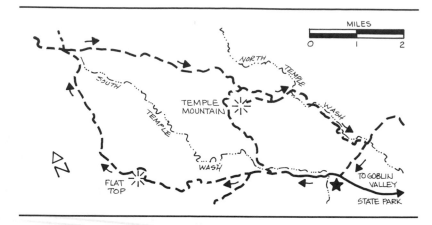

the slopes of Temple Mountain and skirting a wealth of mining artifacts, the road rejoins the narrative below in 0.9 mile, at 13.6.)

Cross a draw at 2.1 and begin climbing steeply, passing a road
forking left. (Note: a good ride itself, this road stretches southwest for
several miles, crossing and providing hiking access into the wonders of
Wild Horse, Crack, and Chute canyons, all within the Crack Canyon
Wilderness Study Area.)

At 2.5 ascend steeply through the eons, represented by layer on
layer of rock strata. The grade temporarily diminishes at 3.0, and at 3.2
you coast past a path forking into a primitive campsite; continue up. At
3.6 pass through a gap in the rock to gain a new perspective on things.
Climb up the big ridge separating two wide drainages, with Flat Top in
front and the cliffs and adjacent mountains of Capitol Reef National
Park on the left in the distance.

At 4.7 skirt the head of a canyon; climb gradually for the next 2.5
miles, with some short, steep grades thrown in for good measure. At
7.2 miles curve left around the head of a draw and resume climbing.
At 8.0, still climbing, enter a high, flat park, decorated with stands of
piñon and juniper. You've climbed above almost everything around;
only Temple Mountain still looms.

At 8.9, before coming to a big mesa on the right, turn hard right
onto the primitive path (at the same point, another road forks left at an
angle of less than 90 degrees). Rolling down through scattered timber,
encounter a stretch of sharp, angular rocks at 9.1. At 9.2 a path curves
right to avoid the worst of the rocks, rejoining the main route in 0.1
mile. As you wind down the terrifically rugged road, aimed straight for
Temple Mountain, spot the distant Abajo and La Sal mountains rising

Temple Mountain Loop samples a cross-section of the diverse reef country.

from the barrens. Hump over a small bump in a red-soil formation at 10.8, then over a little saddle at 11.3 miles; from here, the Henry Mountains are visible to the right. Pass through a shallow rock gap at 12.1 and bear right at 12.6 on the main track as a faint trail goes left. Coast through the draw at 12.7 and commence coasting along its right side. Cross another little draw at 12.9, then curve right to dip through a major wash. Top out at 13.2 and bear left at the fork.

Cross through the big draw at 13.4, push out of it for 100 yards, and at 13.6 miles merge left onto the road coming in from above right. This feeds you onto the top of a low ridge. At 14.1 cross through a draw, curve right, and at 14.3 zoom through a deep draw, passing a dead car on your right. In about 100 yards, bear left/straight onto the road dropping down from the right.

Pass by several old buildings and foundations at 14.4, then coast smoothly. At 15.0 a path forking left accesses a primitive camping area, the first of several passed during the next 3 miles. At 15.8 miles the canyon narrows and the road becomes one with North Temple Wash.

In order to keep up momentum in the thick wash sand/gravel, spin a low gear with lots of *oomph,* and experiment with different lines: some sections are more compacted than others. Riding here is a bit like running in your sleep: your legs are moving, but you seem to be going nowhere. However, there are worse places to be getting nowhere, for this slot canyon is enchanting.

Pass an unusual balancing rock on your left at 17.0; at 17.5 miles curve right, leaving the wash. Coast down through a sandy draw at 18.0 and at 18.4 bear right off the main track, closing the loop at 18.5 miles.

175

48. Cathedral Valley Loop

Riding surface: Pavement and dirt road with sandy stretches
Elevation range: 4,630 to 6,985 feet
Distance: 64.8 miles
Relative difficulty: Moderate
Time to allow: 2 to 3 days
Best time of year: March through May; September to November
Supplemental map: Loa and Salina 1:100,000 metric maps, The Valley of Cathedrals guide map

"Saving the best for last" describes this ride well, for undoubtedly it is the finest multiday mountain-bike outing in the Milky Way galaxy, if not the entire universe. As you cross several distinct geologic formations en route, the spectacles of Capitol Reef, Thousand Lake Mountain, and the namesake sandstone "cathedrals" will keep you enthralled. (Note: an even longer route that takes in Thousand Lake Mountain can be ridden in the fall, after the desert cools and before the snow flies.)

The ride is best accomplished as a vehicle-supported 2- or 3-day loop; only the strongest or most masochistic would dream of completing this ride in 1 day. It can certainly be done self-supported, but each person should carry a minimum of 1 gallon of water per day—resulting in a heavy load when first starting out. Remember, dispersed camping is permitted on BLM lands, but camping is more restricted within the national park portions of the ride.

Before heading out, check in at the Capitol Reef National Park visitor center and let the rangers on duty know what you're up to. They'll have current information on route conditions—for instance, the depth of the mandatory river ford at the ride's beginning. Also find out the weather forecast, for a large share of the road surface is bentonite, which, when wet, becomes slippery and virtually impassable. And pick up a copy of the fine publication entitled *The Valley of Cathedrals*. It contains a map and a running commentary on route highlights relating to numbered "tourstop" markers along the way.

The bentonite and loose sand, the numerous steep climbs, and the extreme distance and remoteness combine to make this an adventure that shouldn't be set out on as a lark. *Advance planning is a requirement.*

From the visitor center at Capitol Reef National Park, go 11.6 miles east on State Highway 24 and turn left at the sign reading "River Ford/Cathedral Valley." In about 0.5 mile, park in the shade of the old cottonwood trees.

Bearing north at the sign reading "Hartnet Road/Bentonite Hills/Cathedral Valley/Thousand Lake Mountain," gingerly walk your bike across the Fremont River. At 0.3 mile switchback left and climb. Top out at 0.9 mile, at tourstop 1. Crest another high point at 1.8 miles and coast down, crossing through a fenceline at 2.3, to a draw crossing at 2.5 miles.

Grand views of the Waterpocket Fold are gained as you proceed northwest, entering North Blue Flats at 4.0. After riding through a couple of sandy draw crossings, at 6.6 miles pass by a cattle spring that is surrounded by tamarisk bushes. At 7.6 begin climbing, very steeply in spots, into the Bentonite, or Rainbow, Hills.

Winding up and down, reach timber at about 9.3 miles. At 9.7 pass a road forking right toward Rock Water and at 10.7 begin climbing into the Hartnet, an expanse of Salt Wash Sandstone that has been eroded into ledges, cliffs, and arroyos. You'll be riding in the Hartnet country for about 15 miles. At 13.0 you ride into and back out of Capitol Reef National Park in a span of 0.25 mile. The road's generally upward trend is interrupted often by short downhills leading to wash crossings.

Forking left at 13.5 is the road leading to Lower South Desert

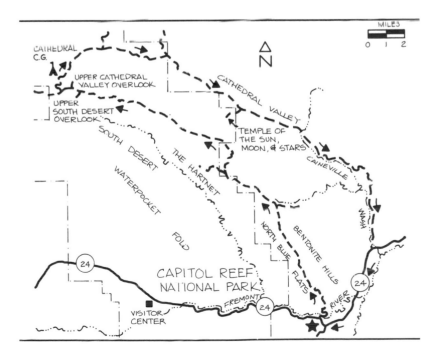

Overlook, a 2.5-mile round trip; continue straight. Cross a cattle guard at 14.3 miles and ride into an area containing a wealth of fine campsites (consider camping here if you're doing a 3-day loop). At 15.8 ride into Capitol Reef National Park and up into a valley protected by sandstone bluffs on either side. On the right at 17.0 is the trailhead for the cross-country hike to Lower Cathedral Valley Overlook.

At 18.5 begin a stretch through the sandstone that dishes up draw crossing after crossing. Enter a deeper rimrock canyon at about 24.0, winding back and forth across the drainage. Climbing above the valley at 24.7, Thousand Lake Mountain now looms very close. At 25.6, near the ridgetop, dismount and walk to the left for a look at the broad South Desert. Keep an eye out for mule deer as you near the mountains.

At 26.6 pass the short road going left to Upper South Desert Overlook; at 26.9 is the road heading right toward Cathedral Valley Overlook. At the junction at 27.4 miles turn right at the sign reading "U-24 26 miles" (straight goes to Thousand Lake Mountain).

At 27.7 is Cathedral Campground, the recommended overnight stop if you're doing the loop in 2 days. At 27.8 start down the mile-

Upper Cathedral Valley, backed by Thousand Lake Mountain

long series of switchbacks leading to the fascinating monoliths of Entrada Sandstone in Upper Cathedral Valley. Bottom out in a draw at 29.4 miles; on the right at 31.2 are the Walls of Jericho, Basilica, and Wall Street features.

Cross through the draw several times during the next mile and pass through a fenceline at 32.2 miles. At the junction at 32.5 head straight at the sign reading "U-24 20 miles" (left goes to Baker Ranch and Interstate 70). At 32.6 the road leading the 1.2 miles to Gypsum Sinkhole goes right. (It's fun to look at, but getting too close to the edge of the sinkhole is dangerous; exploring in it is not permitted without an okay from the NPS.)

Pass through a fenceline at 32.9 and brush against a cathedral on your left. Cross back and forth over the draw several times beginning at 34.9, then climb onto the mesa at 35.3 miles. Go through a sandy draw at 36.3, climb out, and at 36.8 bear right at the junction toward Lower Cathedral Valley, leaving Capitol Reef National Park.

At 40.4 ride onto NPS land for 0.25 mile, then back onto BLM land. At 42.0 a spur road leads right toward Lower Cathedral Valley and the temples of the Sun, the Moon, and the Stars. At 44.1 a primitive track forks right; stretches of deep, loose sand follow.

Cross through a draw bottom at 45.7 miles and climb, then coast into the sandstone valley of Caineville Wash at 46.2. At 46.6 curve right to be greeted with first-class views of the Henrys and the Waterpocket Fold. Pass tourpost 24 (Willow Seep) at 49.4 and tourpost 25 (Queen of the Wash) at 49.9 miles.

Just when you thought it was all downhill from here, begin a 4-mile stretch of incredibly jumbled sandstone ledges and arroyos: up and down, up and down, up and down. (For a 3-day outing, this area is recommended for overnight number two.) Descend from the ridgetop, coasting into a bentonite canyon at 53.9 miles. You soon encounter some sandy stretches; at 55.2 brush against the cliff on the left side of the wash. Crest a high point at 55.7 and spot the highway ahead, on its westward climb.

At 57.4 cross a cattle guard and turn right onto State Highway 24. Entering another mass of intriguing geology, you crest three distinct ridges, including Caineville Reef, during the next 7 miles. Top out at 58.9 and coast down for 1 mile; resume climbing once you're across the Fremont River, at 60.6 miles.

Hit the top at 61.6 and spot the Waterpocket Fold with its mountainous backdrop. After running out the downhill, *again* begin climbing at 63.3 miles. At 64.3, nearing the bottom of the final descent, turn right toward the river ford and return to the ride's beginning point at 64.8 miles.

Other Rides in Utah

Perhaps by now you're convinced that Utah truly *is* the Bicycle Capital of the United States. Even if you aren't prepared to go that far, you probably will agree that its southeastern quadrant warrants further investigation.

Moab area. Popular Moab-area outings—in addition to those featured —include the Moab Rim and Pritchett Canyon rides, both of which fork off the paved road leading down the Colorado River toward Hurrah Pass and penetrate the surrealistic-looking Behind the Rocks area. In the La Sal Mountains, east of town, are terrific rides such as the Porcupine Rim, Onion Creek, Fisher Mesa, Geyser Pass, and tough Burro Pass trails. North and west of town are such highly regarded routes as the Monitor-Merrimac Trail, Poison Spider Mesa, and the renowned White Rim Trail.

The latter is a 100-mile loop—all but a quarter of it within Canyonlands National Park—that begins high on Island in the Sky, then quickly plunges down the Schafer Trail onto the White Rim Sandstone bench, which is midway in elevation between the Island and the canyon bottoms. For 70 miles the White Rim Trail winds above the downstream path of the Colorado River and up the path of the Green River. It then climbs back onto the high plateau via the switchbacks of the Horsethief Trail.

Before heading out on this trip, typically accomplished in 3 or 4 days and with vehicle support, contact the NPS' Moab Headquarters Office, 125 West 200 South, Moab, UT 84532, (801) 259-7164. Because of the trail's popularity among cycling and four-wheel-drive enthusiasts, reservations must be made for the designated campgrounds along the way.

In the planning stages at this writing is a trail spanning the remarkable country between Moab and Natural Bridges National Monument. Envisioned in the tradition of the Kokopelli's Trail, it should be a gem. Information on this and other Moab-area trails is available at the USFS, BLM, and NPS offices and at bikes shops in town.

Canyon Rims Recreation Area. From a few miles north of the turnoff to the road leading into the Needles District of Canyonlands National Park, a paved road leaves U.S. Highway 191 and heads west into the BLM-managed Canyon Rims Recreation Area. From Wind Whistle and Hatch campgrounds, graded roads or jeep trails lead to spots such as Needles Overlook, Jail Rock, Trough Springs Canyon, and Anticline

Overlook. Information on these and other nearby routes suitable for mountain biking is available at the BLM office in Moab.

Abajo Mountains. The Abajo, or Blue, Mountains, visible from many of the featured low-lying rides, offer terrific summer and fall riding. From near Natural Bridges National Monument a road heads northeast over Bears Ears Pass, then splits. One fork winds northwest toward Hite Crossing, another climbs along a high ridge overlooking the Dark Canyon Wilderness Area, and the primary path leads north onto Elk Ridge. From here you can continue northwest through Beef Basin and into the Needles District of Canyonlands (and over infamous Elephant Hill, which also is part of a popular short loop beginning and ending at the Needles' Squaw Flat Campground), northeast down Cottonwood Creek to Dugout Ranch, or east/southeast to wind through the Abajos, finally dropping down into Blanding or Monticello. Various spurs accessing places such as Salt Creek Mesa and Seven Sisters Buttes provide terrific views into the Salt Creek, Davis, and Lavender canyons of the Needles District.

Additional information is available through the Manti-La Sal National Forest, Monticello Ranger District, Monticello, UT 84535 (801) 587-2041 and through previously mentioned NPS and BLM offices.

Canyonlands National Park. In the Maze District of Canyonlands National Park, it's possible to drop off the high rim, via the Flint Trail (see rides 41 and 42), to the Maze Overlook (about a 70-mile round trip from the Hans Flat ranger station) and to the Land of Standing Rocks and the Doll House (approximately 80 miles round trip from the ranger station). These rides are advisably done with four-wheel-drive-vehicle support; a backcountry camping permit, available at the ranger station, is required for camping in the Maze District.

Henry Mountains. Some terrific outings can be found in the remote and little-visited Henry Mountains, home to the last free-ranging bison herd in America. In 1941, 18 head were transported to the Henrys from Yellowstone National Park; they flourished, and today the herd numbers more than 200.

A road beginning at the Little Egypt Geologic Site, approximately 20 miles south of Hanksville on State Highway 95, leads west into the Henrys. It provides access to the road leading over Bull Creek Pass, which can be turned into a loop or a point-to-point ride ending in Capitol Reef National Park. Or, from west of Little Egypt you can follow the road leading south, along the eastern flanks of 11,320-foot Mount Pennell, to Starr Springs Campground. Obtain the General Recreation Map for the Henrys through the Bureau of Land Management Henry Mountains Resource Area, P.O. Box 99, Hanksville, UT 84734, (801) 542-3461.

Glen Canyon Recreation Area. Three extremely remote rides in the Glen Canyon Recreation Area include the Hole-in-the-Rock Road, which leads southwest beneath the Straight Cliffs for 65 miles from the town of Escalante to Lake Powell, and the 25-mile road leading to the lake via Cottonwood Canyon from east of Halls Crossing. These two roads hit the river immediately opposite one another. Also, from Hans Flat the Flint Trail (see rides 41 and 42) continues through the National Recreation Area to Hite Crossing, a distance of more than 100 miles. These all are jeep trails, very hot and dry in summer, and should be attempted only with careful advanced planning—and, advisably, vehicle support. For further details, contact Glen Canyon National Recreation Area, P.O. Box 1507, Page, AZ 86040.

Boulder Mountain area. The mountains ringing the west side of Capitol Reef National Park contain limitless summer riding opportunities. One of the most popular rides in Utah is the spectacular Burr Trail Road, which, beginning in the town of Boulder, crosses BLM lands and then zips through the Waterpocket Fold and into the southern end of Capitol Reef National Park. From here, you can turn onto the Notom-Bullfrog Road and go north to State Highway 24 or south to Bullfrog Marina, on Lake Powell. Ride it soon, for the delightfully rustic Burr is in imminent danger of being graded and improved.

Another outstanding option is the route that begins atop Boulder Mountain, a high-elevation playground in the Dixie National Forest. Actually an extension of the Aquarius Plateau, the mountain's flat "summit" covers 80 square miles. Begin riding near Pleasant Creek Campground, along Forest Road 569/State Highway 12. Heading east, the route follows forest roads 181 and 168, dropping down Pleasant Creek and South Draw to join Scenic Drive in Capitol Reef National Park, at a point approximately 10 miles south of the visitor center. Offering terrific wooded backcountry and vistas of Capitol Reef, the ride loses about 3,000 feet of elevation and can be done as a point-to-point or as a large loop.

Fishlake National Forest. To the north, in the Fishlake National Forest, good mountain-biking opportunities await in the Thousand Lake

Mountain, Gooseberry, and Fish Lake areas, which lie west of Cathedral Valley (see ride 48) and the San Rafael Swell. Rides in these areas and in portions of the forest farther west are described in *Mountain Bicycle Trails on the Fishlake National Forest*, published and distributed by the forest.

Get the Dixie National Forest visitors map (Powell, Escalante, and Teasdale ranger districts) through the Forest Supervisor's Office, P.O. Box 580, Cedar City, UT 84720, (801) 586-2421, and at district offices in Escalante, Panguitch, and Teasdale. The Fishlake National Forest visitors map and the mountain-bike publication are available through the Forest Supervisor's Office, 115 East 900 North, Richfield, UT 84701, (801) 584-8292, and at district offices in Beaver, Fillmore, and Loa.

San Rafael Reef/Swell. As you know if you accomplished rides 16 and 47, the San Rafael Reef/Swell country has much to offer mountain bikers. Other suggested roads and/or destinations include Swasey's Cabin, Copper-Globe Road, Hidden Splendor, Hondoo Arch, and Keesle Country, all south of Interstate 70. North of the interstate, seek out the Wedge Overlook, Swasey's Leap/Mexican Bend, Black Dragon Wash, and Sid's Mountain/Dutchman's Arch. For maps and information, contact the Bureau of Land Management San Rafael Resource Area, 700 East 900 North, Price, UT 84501, (801) 637-4584.

Appendices

A. Recommended Reading

Mountain Biking

All-Terrain Bikes, by the editors of *Bicycling* magazine, Rodale Press, 1985.

Beyond Slickrock: Rides to Nowhere, by Todd Campbell, Rim Tours Publications, 1987.

Bicycle Routes in the San Juan National Forest, San Juan National Forest, 1988.

Bicycle Utah Vacation Guide, P.O. Box 738, Park City, UT 84060, (801) 649-5806. Free publication outlining road-riding and mountain-biking opportunities in the state.

Bicycling the Backcountry—A Mountain Bike Guide to Colorado, by William L. Stoehr, Pruett Publishing, 1987.

Bicycling the Uncompahgre Plateau, by Bill Harris, Wayfinder Press, 1988.

Canyon Country Mountain Biking, by F. A. Barnes and Tom Keuhne, Canyon Country Publications, 1988.

The Cyclists' Yellow Pages, Bikecentennial Publications, 1990. A resource guide for the bicyclist; includes several pages of mountain-biking information.

Eugene Sloane's Complete Book of All-Terrain Bicycles, by Eugene A. Sloane, Simon & Schuster, 1985.

Mountain Bicycle Trails on the Fishlake National Forest, Fishlake National Forest, 1989.

Mountain Bike Adventures in the Northern Rockies, by Michael McCoy, Mountaineers Books, 1989.

Mountain Bike Adventures in Washington's North Cascades and Olympics, by Tom Kirkendall, Mountaineers Books, 1989.

Mountain Bike Adventures in Washington's South Cascades and Puget Sound, by Tom Kirkendall, Mountaineers Books, 1989.

Mountain Biking the Wasatch and Uintas, by Gregg Bromka, Wasatch Book Distribution, 1990.

Richard's Mountain Bike Book, by Charles Kelly, Random House, 1988.

General Bicycling

The Bike Bag Book, by Tom Cuthbertson, Ten Speed Press, 1981. A good one to carry along while riding, in case of mechanical problems.

The Complete Book of Bicycling, by Eugene A. Sloane, Simon & Schuster, 1988.

Freewheeling: Bicycling the Open Road, by Gary Ferguson, Mountaineers Books, 1984. Good general information, much of it adaptable to mountain biking.

Richard's Bicycle Book, by Richard Ballantine, Random House, 1982. A guide to maintenance and repair.

Richard's Cycling for Fitness, by John Schubert, Random House, 1988.

First Aid

Mountaineering First Aid, by M T ento, S. Macdonald, J. Carline, Mountaineers Books, 1985.

Mountaineering Medicine, by Fred T. Darvill, M.D., Wilderness Press, 1983.

Standard First Aid and Personal Safety, by the American Red Cross, Doubleday & Co., 1979.

Mountaineering and Camping

Be An Expert with Map and Compass, by Bjorn Kjellstrom, American Orienteering Service, 1976.

Mountaineering—The Freedom of the Hills, edited by Ed Peters, Mountaineers Books, 1982. Largely concerned with climbing, this book contains basics that every outdoors enthusiast should be familiar with.

Rand McNally RV Park and Campground Directory: U.S., Canada, and Mexico, Rand McNally & Co., 1988. Information-packed directory that includes listings of both private and public camp grounds.

Natural History

Audubon Field Guide to North American Birds, Western Region.
Cañons of the Colorado, by Major John Wesley Powell.
Deserts—Audubon Society Nature Guide, by James A. MacMahon.
Flowers of the Southwest Deserts, by Natt N. Dodge.
Flowers of the Southwest Mountains, by L. Arnberger and J. Janish.

Shrubs and Trees of the Southwest Uplands, by Francis Elmore.
Western Forests, by Stephen Whitney, Alfred A. Knopf, 1985.

*Available through the Canyonlands Natural History Association, 125 West 200 South, Moab, UT 84532, (801) 259-6003.

Archaeology and Geology

Anasazi, Ancient People of the Rock, by D. Pike and D. Muench.
Ancient Ruins of the Southwest, by David Noble.
The Colorado Plateau—A Geologic History, by Donald L. Baars, University of New Mexico Press, 1983.
The Delight Makers, by Adolph Bandelier, Harcourt Brace Jovanovich, Inc., 1971.
Images on Stone—Prehistoric Rock Art of the Colorado Plateau, by Donald Weaver, Jr.
Pages of Stone: Geology of Western National Parks and Monuments, by Halka Chronic, Mountaineers Books. "The Desert Southwest" and "Grand Canyon and Plateau Country" editions.
Roadside Geology series, Mountain Press. Individual state volumes available.
Those Who Came Before, by R. and F. Lister.

*Available through the Canyonlands Natural History Association, 125 West 200 South, Moab, UT 84532, (801) 259-6003.

Diet and Cookbooks

Cycle Food: A Guide to Satisfying Your Inner Tube, by Lauren Hefferon, Ten Speed Press, 1983.
NOLS Cookery, by the National Outdoor Leadership School, Emporia State Press, 1980.

B. Additional Map and Information Sources

Arizona Office of Tourism, 1480 East Bethany Home Road, Phoenix, AZ 85014, (602) 255-3618.

Bikecentennial, P.O. Box 8308-MM, Missoula, MT 59807, (406) 721-1776. Specializes in cycling books and maps.

Bureau of Land Management, Department of the Interior, Office of Public Affairs, 18th & C Street Northwest, Washington, DC 20240, (202) 343-5717. Maps covering all lands administered by the Bureau of Land Management.

Colorado Tourism Board, 1625 Broadway, Suite 1700, Denver, CO 80203, (800) 433-2656.

Distribution Branch, U.S. Geological Survey, Box 25286, Federal Center Building 41, Denver, CO 80225, (303) 236-7477. Ask for key locating U.S. Geological Survey topographic maps.

Four Corners Tourism Council, P.O. Box 540, Mancos, CO 81328.

New Mexico Tourism Department, 1100 St. Francis Drive, Santa Fe, NM 87503, (505) 827-0300.

Superintendent of Documents, U.S. Government Printing Office, Washington, DC 20402. Sells map and key to all lands administered by the National Park Service.

Utah Travel Council, Council Hall, Capitol Hill, Salt Lake City, UT 84114, (801) 538-1030.

C. Mail-order Equipment

Bikecology, 1515 Wilshire, Santa Monica, CA 90403.
Bike Nashbar, 4111 Simon, Youngstown, OH 44512.
Campmor, P.O. Box 998, Paramus, NJ 07653.
Cycle Goods, 2735 Hennepin Avenue South, Minneapolis, MN
    55408.
Eastern Mountain Sports, Vose Farm Road, Peterborough, NH
    03458.
Eddie Bauer, Box 3700, Seattle, WA 98124.
L. L. Bean, Freeport, ME 04032.
Mountain Bike Specialists, 346 South Camino del Rio, Durango, CO
    81301
Recreational Equipment, Inc., P.O. Box C-88125, Seattle, WA
    98188-0125.

MICHAEL McCOY lives in Missoula, Montana, where he is the trips director for BikeCentennial and an editorial assistant for *BikeReport*. He is author of *Mountain Bike Adventures in the Northern Rockies* (The Mountaineers), and his articles and photographs have appeared in *Bicycling, Bicycle Guide*, and *Southwest Cycling*. McCoy spent a large part of his youth barreling down hills on his two-speed Schwinn "Tiger."

INDEX

Abajo Mountains, 138, 148, 154, 161, 163, 166, 174, 181
Abert's squirrel, 48, 67
Albuquerque, 122, 124, 136
All-American Man, 152, 154
Alpine Plateau, 103
American Basin, 102
Anasazis, 119, 151–54, 161, 166, 168
Angel Arch, 151–54
Angel Arch Campground, 152, 154
Animas Forks, 102
Apache Trail, 32, 35
Arches National Park, 140–42, 144
Arizona Trail, 67
Aspen, 75, 78
Avery Peak Campground, 79

Baca Location 1, 118, 123, 126
Bachelor Cove Campground, 36
Bandelier, Adolf, 123
Bandelier National Monument, 123
Bandelier Tuff, 119, 122
Barnhardt Mesa, 40
Barnhardt Trailhead, 39, 40
Bates Wilson Campground, 152
Bear Wallow Canyon, 57
Bears Ears, 166, 181
Beaver Creek Reservoir, 97
Behind the Rocks, 144, 180
Bentonite Hills, 177–79
Bermuda Flat Campground, 35
Bikecentennial, 21, 187
Bishops Lodge, 107, 109
Black Ridge, 71
Bluff, 161, 166
Boulder Mountain, 182
Brazos Mountains, 129–33
Bullfrog Marina, 182

Burned Mountain, 131–33
Burr Point, 158, 160
Burr Trail, 182
Burro Pass Trail, 180
Butler Wash, 165–68
Butler Wash Indian Ruins, 168

Camp Verde, 50
Cañon de San Diego, 119, 124, 133
Canyon Rims Recreation Area, 180–81
Cape Solitude, 64–66, 68
Capitol Reef National Park, 169–79, 174, 176–79, 181, 182–83
Capulin Campground, 116
Carson Trail, 101–2
Castle Mountain, 82
Cathedral Campground, 178
Cathedral Valley, 172, 176–80, 183
Cebolla Mesa, 117–18
Cedar Mesa, 163–65
Cement Creek, 82, 84–85
Cement Creek Campground, 84
Cerro Pelado, 118, 124–27
Chama River Wilderness, 133, 134
Chimney Rock Anasazi Ruins, 93
Cholla Bay Campground, 35
Cinnamon Pass, 101, 103
Clear Creek Campground, 50
Cleopatra's Chair, 157
Coal Bank Pass, 85, 86
Cochiti Pueblo, 119, 121, 123
Collegiate Peaks, 84
Colorado National Monument, 71, 72
Colorado Plateau, 11, 46, 169
Colorado Trail, 100
Colter, Mary Jane, 65

Comb Ridge, 161, 165–68
Crack Canyon WSA, 170, 174
Creede, 93, 101
Crested Butte, 69, 75–85
Cross Creek Campground, 97, 100
Cryptogam, 22, 24, 139
Curecanti NRA, 103
Cypress Thicket, 41–42

Damfino Creek, 56, 57
Desert View, 64
Desert View Watch Tower, 64, 65
Devils Windpipe, 50
Diamond Point Lookout, 43, 44
Diné, 12, 161
Dirty Devil River, 157, 158–60
Doll House, 181
Dolores, 104
Durango, 69, 85, 100

East River, 79, 81
El Cabezon, 134–35
Elephant Hill, 181
El Malpais, 135–36
El Vallecito Ranch, 131, 132
Engineer Mountain, 86
Engineer Pass, 101, 103

Farmington, 136
Fat Tire Bike Week, 76
Fat Tire Commandments, 21
Fernando Mountains, 114–16
First-aid kit, 20
Fish Lake, 182-83
Flagstaff, 39, 48, 56, 60–63
Flint Trail, 156, 158, 181, 182
Four Corners Region, 11, 61, 129
Four Peaks Wilderness Area, 36, 37
Fremont Indians, 151, 173

Garcia Park, 115
Gemini Bridges, 142–44
Giardiasis, 28
Glen Canyon NRA, 147–48,
    154–58, 182

Goblin Valley State Park, 170–71,
    173
Goosenecks State Park, 161, 163
Gothic, 78–80
Gothic Peak Campground, 79
Grand Canyon, 31, 49, 60, 61,
    64–66, 67
Grand Junction, 71–75
Grants, 124, 136
Grayrock Peak, 89
Graysill, 87–90
Graysill Mountain, 89
Great Sand Dunes National
    Monument, 104

Hanksville, 159, 160, 181
Hans Flat Ranger Station, 148,
    156, 181
Hartnet, 177–79
Henry Mountains, 138, 143, 156,
    160, 163, 171, 172, 175, 181
Hermosa, 91, 93
Hermosa Creek, 90–93
High Road to Taos, 111
Hite Crossing, 181, 182
Hole in the Rock Trail, 161, 166
Hopewell Ridge, 132–33
Hopewell Lake Campground, 132
Horses, 21
Horse Thief Trail, 180
Hovenweep National Monument,
    161
Hurrah Pass, 144–47, 180
Hyde Park Road, 107, 108

Imogene Pass, 102
Island in the Sky, 144, 148, 149,
    154, 180

Javelina, 35
Jemez Mountains, 118–29
Jemez Springs, 124, 127
Jerome, 53–54, 58, 59
Jumbo Campground, 74

Kachina Peaks Wilderness, 62
Kaibab squirrel, 49, 67
Kissing Camels, 151
Kokopelli's Trail, 70, 101, 139, 180

La Junta Point, 118
Lake City, 93, 101–2
Land of Standing Rocks, 154, 181
Lands End, Colorado, 73–75, 157
Lands End, Utah, 157–58
La Patecas Campground, 116
La Sal Mountains, 138, 143, 144,
   148, 154, 174, 180
La Sombra Campground, 116
Lime Creek, 85–87
Little Colorado River, 65, 66, 68
Little Egypt Geologic Site, 181–82
Little Wild Horse Canyon, 170–72
Lone Pine Saddle, 38
Los Alamos, 119

Maestas Park, 113
Mazatzal Mountains, 31–38, 39,
   40, 42
Mazatzal Wilderness, 39, 40, 47
Maze District, 154, 157, 181
Mesa, 37, 68
Mexican Hat, 161, 165
Mingus Mountain, 54, 58–59
Moab, 103, 137–47, 180
Mogollon Rim, 38, 42, 43, 45,
   46–53, 57
Moki Dugway, 163
Momaday, N. Scott, 119
Monitor-Merrimac Trail, 180
Monticello, 149, 181
Monument Valley, 161, 163, 165
Mountain Bike Hall of Fame, 76
Mount Crested Butte, 78, 80
Mount Elden Lookout, 61–63
Muley Point, 163
Munds Mountain Wilderness Area,
   57
Museum of Northern Arizona, 61,
   62

Museum of Western Colorado, 70

Natural Bridges National
   Monument, 166, 180, 181
Navajo Reservation, 12, 66, 161
Needles District, 147–54, 181, 182
Newspaper Rock, 149
North Kaibab Ranger District, 67
No-trace camping, 24
Nunatak, 87

Oak Creek, 57
Oak Creek Canyon, 53, 56–58, 60
Oak Hill, 50–53
Obsidian Ridge, 122–24
Odometers, 17
Oh Be Joyful Creek, 76–78
Ojito, 134–35
Optimum Riding Months chart, 25
Ouray, 102–3

Packer, Alferd, 102
Pagosa Springs, 93–100, 103–4
Painted Desert, 65
Pajarito Plateau, 118, 123
Palace of the Governors, 105–6
Palatki Ruins, 68
Panorama Point, 154–57
Paradise Divide, 80
Paul Bunyan's Potty, 152
Payson, 38–45, 47
Pearl Pass, 75–76, 81, 82
Pecos National Monument, 133
Peekaboo Spring, 152, 153
Pine, 47, 68
Poage Lake, 97, 100
Porcupine Rim, 180
Potato Patch Campground, 59
Powderhorn ski area, 75
Powell, John Wesley, 12, 159
Pritchett Canyon Trail, 146, 180
Pueblo Indians, 105, 106
Purgatory, 85–93
Purgatory Campground, 86, 89, 91

Ranchos de Taos, 112, 115
Rattlesnakes, 27
Redondo Campground, 124
Redondo Peak, 124, 129
Red River, 117–18
Rio Chiquito, 114–16
Rio Grande del Rancho, 114
Rocky Mountain Biological
    Laboratory, 78
Rye, 40–43

Salt Creek, 149, 151–54, 181
San Antonio Campground, 127–8
San Francisco Peaks, 52
Sangre de Cristos, 106–9, 124
San Juan Mountains, 96, 101–2,
    154
San Juan Triangle, 101–2
San Rafael Reef, 169–75, 183
San Rafael Swell, 169–75, 183
Santa Fe, 105–9, 111, 124, 133
Schnebly Hill Vista, 56, 58
Schofield Pass, 79
Schultz Creek Trail, 62
Secret Canyon, 54, 55
Secret Mountain Wilderness, 55
Sedona, 53–58, 68
Show Low, 68
Sierra de Don Fernando, 116
Sig Creek Campground, 89, 90
Silverton, 103
Slate River, 78, 80
Slickrock Bike Trail, 17, 138–39
Sons of the Pioneers, 117
South Fork, 93–100
Spring Creek, 129–31
Squaw Flat Campground, 148, 181
Superstition Mountains, 31–38, 68
Superstition Wilderness, 32, 35

Talpa, 112, 115
Taos, 110–18, 134
Telluride, 102–3
Temple Mountain, 173–75
Ten Essentials, 20

Tent Rocks SMA, 135
Teocalli Ridge, 81–83
Tesuque Indian Reservation, 107
Theodore Roosevelt Lake, 31, 35,
    36, 68
Thousand Lake Mountain, 172,
    176–79, 182–83
Tires, 15
Tonto Creek Campground, 43, 45
Tonto National Monument, 32
Topographic maps, 14
Tortilla Flat, 34
Trail of the Ancients, 161–68
Tres Piedras, 129, 130
Tusas Box Canyon, 130
Tusas Mountains, 129–33
Tusayan Ranger District, 67
Tuzigoot National Monument, 58

Uncompahgre Plateau, 70, 71, 74,
    101, 184

Valle Grande Caldera, 118, 124
Valley of the Gods, 163–65
Verde River Valley, 50, 54, 56, 58,
    59
Vultee Arch, 54, 55

Wagon Wheel Gap, 101
Walnut Canyon Game Enclosure,
    35
Waterpocket Fold, 169, 177, 179,
    182
Weather, 24–25
West Clear Creek Wilderness Area,
    49
Wheeler Geologic Area, 101
White Rim Trail, 148, 151, 180
Williams District, 67
Willow Draw, 95–96
Winsor Trail, 107–9
Wolf Creek Pass, 93
Woodchute Wilderness, 58
Wupatki National Monument, 68

Zane Grey Cabin, 43, 45